Alone Together

Voices of Single Mothers

edited by Jenny Morris

The Women's Press

First published in Great Britain by The Women's Press Limited
A member of the Namara Group
34 Great Sutton Street,
London EC1V 0DX.

British Library Cataloguing in Publication Data:
A catalogue record of this book is available from the British Library

ISBN 0 7043 4293 6

Typeset by Contour Typesetters, Southall, London
Printed and bound in Great Britain by
BPCC Hazells Ltd.
Member of BPCC Ltd.

Contents

To Rosa Kate Morris

Acknowledgments

Thank you to my daughter, Rosa, who drew the picture for the front cover. We wanted a picture which would, at first sight, look as if it was a stereotypical family, so Rosa had to be persuaded to draw a mother who wasn't in a wheelchair. She also commented, 'Why does this picture only have white people in it?'

Rosa also thought of the title, for which we were all very grateful, as we had spent months trying to think of one.

My thanks to all the contributors for the emotional effort which went into writing each piece. And also to those children who read their mothers' writing and were willing for their experiences to be shared with others.

This book was a joy to put together because the women who contributed shared their experiences so generously, and thus made possible a collection of writings about the many different kinds of ways in which women experience being a single mother.

Introduction

In all the public representations of the 'problem of single mothers', the voice of the mothers themselves is noticeably absent. Neither do most of the public representations of motherhood include single motherhood. Our experience is set apart, made different and deviant, defined by our social and economic status.

Single mothers are publicly presented as poor, as struggling, as unhappy, as oppressed. Some or all of these may be features of our lives but the way in which we 'appear' in public objectifies us because it is not we who define our lives but others who do – in their role as politicians, journalists, health and social services professionals, and social scientists. We are turned into objects defined by other people's perceptions of our lives. This is how we come to be viewed as a 'social problem'.

This book is motivated by the feminist goal of creating a space where women can present themselves in their own terms, of giving a voice to an experience which is too often absent from the cultural representations of motherhood. It is not motivated by the wish to present a 'positive image' of single motherhood. I am not sure what a 'positive image' is. I do know that often attempts to portray such an image only serve to make women feel inadequate, often only provide yet another standard which we feel we cannot live up to.

In compiling this book, I have also been motivated by having a fairly clear idea about the kind of books which I enjoy reading. I want to read about what happens to people.

It is a myth that most people's lives follow a set, familiar pattern. Behind the façade of seeming ordinariness are interesting events, fascinating experiences. I also want to read about what people feel about the things which happen to them. Most importantly, I want to read books which, in enabling people to present their lives and their concerns in their own terms, promote a compassionate understanding of our complex humanity.

Compiling this book

Hardly any of the women who have contributed to this book see themselves as writers. Even for the one or two who do, writing about being a single mother was very difficult. I was clear from the start that, if the book were to reflect the huge variety of experience that women bringing up children on their own encounter, then I could not behave as a traditional editor. I could not ask for completed, typed manuscripts delivered by a certain date. Instead my editorial role had to adapt itself to meet the needs of the women whom I wanted to contribute. This meant encouraging contributions in a number of different forms and accepting that most would not meet the deadlines that I set. The initial deadline for first drafts was in fact over a year before the deadline for the completed manuscript – which has meant that the women who did meet the first deadline have had to wait a very long time to see their work in print. Most of the contributors, however, needed many months of extending deadlines.

I also tried not to use the pressure of guilt about failing to do something on time because I didn't want to collude in all those social pressures which sometimes make us feel inadequate as women bringing up children on our own. This was quite difficult as I needed to encourage the contributors to try to meet deadlines at the same time as telling them it was all right if they didn't. As time went on, I did get the impression that some women's hearts sank when they heard my voice on the telephone and I developed my own guilty feelings about being part of the pressure in their lives.

A number of different forms of expression went into the building of the total of seventeen contributions. A small number of women did actually give me typewritten drafts which were more or less complete, but the majority either gave me bits and pieces which they then built up to a whole on the basis of the feedback I gave them, or we used taped transcripts of interviews to create a piece of writing. Whatever the method, the final result is their words and their writing.

My original brief to the contributors was that I wanted them to deal with the events which brought them to the situation of being a single mother, to write about their relationship with their child(ren) and about the factors which affect their parenting. There were many common experiences and themes to emerge from the resulting pieces of writing, in spite of the fact that this book covers such a wide variety of situations. Perhaps the clearest common denominator is the importance of our children in our lives. As Micheline Mason writes, 'Once I had become a parent, I felt as though I had crossed to the other side of an enormous chasm, never to return.' This chasm is created by both the intensity of the relationship with babies and young children *and* by the social and economic consequences of becoming a parent.

My intention in the rest of this introduction is to give an idea of the kind of experiences and feelings that the seventeen contributors have explored in this book.

Becoming a single mother

There were varying degrees of choice involved in the many different situations which led to single parenthood. For Diana Richards, who conceived her son when she was 16, the option of choosing an abortion was inhibited by her reluctance to admit her pregnancy to herself. 'By the time I admitted to myself that I was pregnant I was twelve weeks gone and I felt it was too late to terminate it. It took so long to admit to myself that I was pregnant because I thought my father would kill me.' Her real choice came later on with the decision to keep her child, encouraged by her aunt and her grandmother.

Micheline Mason's pregnancy, at the age of 32, was also not planned, 'being conceived greatly against the odds whilst using contraceptives'. She has brittle bones, an hereditary conditon, and the decision not to seek an abortion did, as she says, take courage. 'I want to take full credit for that . . . I did not even know if I could physically survive a pregnancy, or if the baby would inherit my condition. Once I had made the decision to choose life, and whatever that may bring, the confirmation that the baby did indeed have brittle bones only seemed to make the initial decision more meaningful and special.'

Sheela Bonarjee, whose husband walked out on her and their two small children, did not choose to be a single mother but she did choose to make her children her primary commitment in her life. 'I decided that, if I was going to be left on my own, bringing up the children would be entirely my commitment . . . I think that it gave them strength to know that, even if they had only one parent, they had a truly committed parent.' Sindhu Hope, on the other hand, made a definite decision to leave her husband – 'After years of turmoil and indecision I realised and accepted that I could not both remain in my marriage and be true to myself . . . I had become aware that I was attempting to maintain a situation that nurtured others but not myself.'

A number of contributors asserted a choice within the context of constraints when they left an unhappy relationship. Vivette Ferguson eventually forced her children's father to leave after years of putting up with his relationship with another woman. 'I had got to the stage where, one weekend when he went to see Sandra's parents in Kent, I even packed his bag for him. It felt very therapeutic; every time I put something in the bag it was a little bit of our life that I was putting in there. One morning soon after that, I told him that he had to decide. He should either give me the keys to the flat now and go or he should decide that he was here as a part of this family.'

Maureen Sullivan left her husband in Ireland with the excuse of bringing her two sons to London to help them find work. 'I told my husband I was coming back but I had no intention of doing so. It was quite the best thing I ever did.' For Kate Mariat the flight to a women's refuge with her two small daughters also involved subterfuge. 'I couldn't be sure when we could get away but that didn't seem to matter, we had somewhere to go. He slept downstairs – as if we would slip out in the night. It was a silent contest of wills . . . About a week later I had the opportunity to pick up the bag of nappies that had lain subversively waiting for days, get myself and my two daughters out of the house and to the station, without being seen by anyone we knew.'

For a few contributors, becoming a single mother was the result of a positive choice made in the context of wanting to have a child. I wrote about how, when I came off the pill at the age of 30, 'a desire to have a child hit me with an irresistible force. My menstrual cycle developed into a clear pattern of an overwhelming wish to become pregnant followed by a relief that I hadn't and a fear that I would never be able to cope if I did. I remember, during the weeks of desire for a child, working out in exact detail how I would organise my life to make parenthood possible, while the weeks when the desire had gone felt empty and flat.' Barbara Walker wrote of how, after spending her 20s and early 30s building a career and enjoying a fairly affluent lifestyle, a number of developments in her life made her start to think about having a child. Once she had made the decision to become pregnant, she considered the range of options open to her as a single lesbian and eventually chose to advertise for a sperm donor in *City Limits*. 'The year I became pregnant there were 10,000 artificial insemination by donor births in the USA alone and I reasoned that, although my journey to pregnancy would appear out of the ordinary to some people, by the time my child grew up, the irrepressible tide of women's initiatives towards fulfilment would have widened the availability of choices around conception and motherhood still further.'

Love and vulnerability

Many of us wrote about the shock of the love for a new-born baby. Pippa Murray writes, 'The birth of my first child Jessie, who is now 10, was the most joyfully overwhelming experience of my life. Immediately she was born I felt a huge, unconditional, mutual love begin to grow between us – something I had never experienced before.' Caroline MacKeith's experience of bonding with the 22-month-old child whom she adopted, is echoed by many women in the early months after their child is born. 'I remember that I just wanted to hold her all the time and not do anything else . . . I just wanted to lie in bed with her, play and go for walks with her. I remember around our first Christmas, feeling really starry-eyed and in love and not wanting to do anything else except be with her.'

The intensity of this close relationship with a new baby (or newly adopted child) is often combined with a frightening feeling of vulnerability, something which many new mothers experience but which is heightened by being on your own. Jean Ellis describes how, even while she felt a 'self-sufficiency and sheer contentedness at being alone with my child . . . and the exhilaration of succeeding at what I had set out to do', she yet became fearful and imagined all sorts of disasters happening to her and/or her child. Both sets of emotions had the same source – her love for Daniel. 'I felt overwhelmed by the vision of a lifetime of fear for his physical safety. The fact that my happiness was now tied in with another person's existence was wholly terrifying.'

Being on your own with a small baby often seems to involve contradictory feelings of self-sufficiency and vulnerability. Sindhu Hope writes, 'I loved becoming a mother and on the whole enjoyed having the baby on my own.' And yet she also writes, 'What terrified me . . . was the reality of his dependence on me – the reality of his aloneness without me. Night after night I would dream or fantasise a scenario where I was dead, he was alone and no one knew. He would lie in his cot crying and no one would come.' Most of us have had these fears that something would take us away from our child and for one of us, myself, the nightmare came true – 'A month after Rosa's first birthday . . . something happened to me which is every new mother's nightmare. While Rosa was fast asleep in her cot, I had an accident which permanently disabled me and took me away from her for five months.'

Freedom and pressures

The physical and emotional closeness between a mother and her new-born baby can be excluding of other adults. Sindhu Hope describes how being on her own with her first child was in some ways easier than being married when she had her second. Of the first experience she writes, 'I enjoyed the freedom to immerse myself in providing and caring for him without the conflicting pull of anyone else's needs/demands. I loved the feeling of being a self-contained unit – just the two of us.' In contrast, by the time her second child was born, she was married and she found this situation emotionally far harder – 'I had to cope with the difficulty of fulfilling the expectations and demands of being a wife/lover and mother . . . I was "in love" with my baby and yet I could not immerse myself with her in the way that I had with my first child, because my husband needed/wanted me.'

Sindhu is not alone in feeling such conflicts. Pippa Murray writes about the pressures of parenting with her children's father, 'When I had just had Jessie and we were living with her father, I became aware that I was mothering him emotionally. I didn't want to do that, he couldn't see the problem and so we reached an impasse. I feel much happier now I am not mothering another adult.'

Those women whose marriage or cohabiting relationship broke down when their children were a bit older, often found that they were then able to take a new-found pleasure in nurturing and providing for their children. Kate Mariat writes of how she 'got down to the serious task of parenting – the sheer delight of being able to take charge, structure, regulate and cohere our lives'. Kate also writes of the stresses which sometimes go with being solely responsible for our children's well-being and of the way in which the pressures often leave no room for our own emotional needs – 'During those first two years . . . I was utterly immersed in the mother role, totally preoccupied with day to day coping. I barely noticed that my needs – social, emotional, sexual – went completely unmet, nor, if I got round to thinking about it at all, could I see any way to meet them.'

Often the pressures come from outside, from the public world's scrutiny of us as single mothers. As Kate also says, 'I felt under pressure from all sides to be an exemplary mother (a pressure I had not experienced within the respectability of a destructive marriage) and I knew our survival depended on my compliance.' Eileen Phillips, who, before her daughter was born, would never have been scared of health or social services professionals, reacted with fear when her health visitor accused her of ignoring her daughter's immunisation appointment. 'Instead of responding with all the middle-class outrage I could muster – I had after all decided not to keep the appointment because I wasn't keen on immunisations for illnesses which wouldn't leave permanent damage – I shuffled my feet and promised to go next week. I went . . . because I was scared they might take Ella away from me. The state terrified me and I wasn't used to feeling that scared . . . social workers, health workers, were dangerous for the first time.'

Mary John writes of the difficulties caused by bureaucratic inefficiency and unsympathetic social security officers. 'The DHSS would make you go up and down to their office, make you wait for your money only to tell you that it is in the post and that you will get it the next day. The next day it still hasn't arrived and you would spend the weekend borrowing the money off the women in the (refuge) to feed your children. It would go on like that for weeks until they sent you the money.'

Self-sufficiency and poverty

Most of us have experienced a shortage of money during at least some stage in our lives as parents. The experience of poverty is often an inevitable accompaniment to becoming a single mother, but for some women control over restricted resources brings a feeling of being better off compared to a situation where a husband/partner's behaviour can mean greater insecurity and poverty.

When Sheela Bonarjee's husband left her and her two small children, he not only took his income but also stole all of his wife's savings. 'I had no job, my savings had gone and I had a mortgage of £6,500 – a lot of money in those days (1969). I let out every room in the house, keeping only one room for myself and the children.'

Barbara Walker's choice of single parenthood converted relative affluence into the hard work of earning enough to pay an increased mortgage, bills and £200 per month baby-minding fees. She had to take on private teaching in the evenings and at weekends in addition to her job as a music teacher. She writes, 'for the next two years during termtime I was often numb with exhaustion and became more isolated as the work timetable cut through the usual times when people get together. I bought equipment second-hand, ate a lot of cheese sandwiches and gratefully received large sacks of toddler clothes from friends.'

In contrast, Mary John writes how other people's reactions to her shortage of money upsets her – 'The only problem I've got at the moment is that people offer me clothes and money. If they only knew how much it hurts, I'm sure they wouldn't offer it. I am not working but I will never have to beg.'

Some of us have chosen to live on benefits rather than waged work, particularly when our children are young. Caroline MacKeith made a positive decision to give up her job and become a full-time parent. 'As that first year went on and I was both getting to know Maresa and adjusting to my life as a parent, I found myself getting less interested in my work and the other outside things I was involved with . . . After I had had Maresa for about eighteen months, I hurt my back and needed a lot of help for a few weeks. I decided then to have some more leave from work and during that time I worked out that, taking into account the benefits I could get, I could afford not to work. So I decided to leave my job permanently and I have never regretted that decision.'

Maureen Sullivan found that she was better off once she left her husband in Ireland and came over to London with her six children. 'We had a lot of financial problems at home. My husband wasn't working and hasn't been working for years. It was very difficult, we never had anything and we were usually broke on a Monday . . . We used to survive on getting tick at the shop and it was getting worse and worse. We argued.' Although she is still living on social security benefits, Maureen now says, 'I'm so much better off financially because I've got the money in my pocket. At home I didn't even used to have the money to give the kids to get into the swimming-pool but now I have control over the money.'

Carole Sturdy writes of how a feeling of having to provide for her child gave her permission to have ambitions in terms of a career. '. . . being a single parent was also a way for me of resolving a long-standing conflict which, put crudely, had been between being 'hard-headed', using my brain, and giving more importance to the world of feelings and interpersonal relations. Being a single parent was a way of being, of *having* to be both, since I had both to support Ciaran and care for him. It gave me permission to have ambition, to strive for success, without sacrificing, through my role as a mother, the world of domesticity and feelings. Being a single parent was a way of *having* to have it both ways in a sense that may not necessarily have been the case if I had been a mother in a conventional nuclear family.'

Public services and private lives

The restrictions on our earning power, which being alone with small children brings, also means that public services – housing, transport, education – can make a major impact on the quality of our lives because we often cannot afford to pay for such things. One of the reasons why Maureen's life improved so much when she left her husband was that she was able to get a five-bedroom council house, suitable for her youngest daughter's disability, and to rely on local authority services such as transport to a special school. Her surprise at the good quality of the house she was offered illustrates our more common unsatisfactory experience of public services. 'When I first came down to see the house where I'm now living, I was looking all around and I couldn't see which house it could be. All the houses looked like they were private, not like council houses. I was so surprised when I saw it. I didn't think it would be as big as this. I didn't think a council place could be like this.'

Public services which are intended to be supportive can sometimes be unhelpful. Kate Mariat describes her experience of being referred to a child guidance clinic with her daughters which was, she says, 'like a trial without a charge. I simply had to interact with my children and answer the odd question, while one "magistrate" made copious notes and the other observed our every move. It was an intimidating set up.' Although she explained that she thought the source of her elder daughter's unhappiness was the access visits to her father, '. . . they were quite dismissive. Perhaps the problem was me. The imposition of this unspoken doubt was unnecessary and caused additional stress at a time when I needed support.'

Both Kate Mariat and Mary John relied on women's aid refuges, a resource made possible by the women's movement, to enable them to leave their husband/boyfriend. Mary wrote, 'Anyone who hasn't been to a refuge does not know the courage it takes to walk out of your home, family and friends.'

Inadequacies in public services and the stereotyping of single mothers by some health and social services professionals can have a significant impact on our lives – and our vulnerability to such inadequacies and stereotyping is, of course, increased by the experience of poverty.

Disabling society

When a child is disabled the inadequacies of the public services and the attitudes of health and social services professionals can result in even greater calls on a mother's energies. Micheline Mason (whose daughter, like her, has brittle bones) has had to become her own expert on researching and resourcing the assistance which she and her daughter require. 'The initiative I have had to have in order to manage my life with Lucy has been a never ending necessity because, it seems, no one can imagine or work out in advance the fact that we will need assistance to do such and such a thing, or that we might be in a state of urgent need, unless I constantly spell it out . . . Seven years on a tightrope and many more to come. There must be better ways in which communities can work together than this.'

Pippa Murray's fight for a better quality life for her brain-injured son is constricted by the unhelpful stereotyping which is applied to her as a mother. She has been labelled as having a 'separation problem' because she did not want to leave her 8-year-old son in a hospital 200 miles away from home and is reluctant to send him to a boarding school. She writes, 'I find it difficult to accept that Kim is being treated as something other than an 8-year-old child. He is *not* "an epileptic", he is a child who has epileptic fits. Of course I have a "separation" problem about the idea of my 8-year-old child going away to boarding school . . . He's like any other child. He breathes, he bleeds when he falls over, he's happy, he's sad. I find it very destructive when the label that is applied to him comes before his humanity.'

Stereotyping is too often the only way in which disability is made visible. Within mainstream education, however, disabled children and parents are discriminated against by a general refusal to recognise their existence at all. As a disabled parent, I have found myself caught between my anger at such discrimination exercised by my daughter's primary school against disabled children and parents and the fact that, on other measures, it is a 'good' school and Rosa enjoys going there. 'I have to move carefully between my anger that this September she will have to move upstairs and I will no longer be able to visit her classroom, my despair that other children have harassed her because her class has been kept downstairs for two years longer than it would otherwise, Rosa's conflicting feelings about moving upstairs and my wish that school should remain a positive experience for her.'

Racism

Sheela Bonarjee first encountered racism when she was running an accommodation agency in London in the 1960s. She was determined to do her utmost to protect her children from such prejudice and to this end she insisted that her children take her ex-husband's English name in order that they would be treated as non-Asian. 'Neither of the children looks particularly Asian, so having the name Bonarjee was what really identified them as Asian . . . I feel we live in an unfair and unjust world and we have to wear the gloves for it.'

Angela Jules did not feel that her daughter experienced racism at her, mainly white, primary school but she was perturbed to discover that there was research showing that West Indian children underachieved at British schools. 'I was really shocked because this wasn't my perception at all. I found it very worrying.' This concern partly motivated her decision to send her daughter to a fee-paying school, run on the West Indian principles of education. 'This means that there are exams every term and that if the child doesn't pass the end of year exams they have to repeat the year. It's very strict and does all the things I hated at school in the West Indies but now I realise how much better the educational standards are there.'

Jean Ellis, as the white mother of a black child, is very aware of the importance of both giving her son positive connections with his African origins and tackling his experience of growing up as a black child in a white, racist society. She writes, 'He has been fortunate in having little direct experience of racism, but this has not occurred without effort. His school was chosen with care. I ran a mile from one where the headteacher referred me to the remedial teacher when I asked about multi-cultural education.' Jean does feel, however, that had Daniel's father been around he might have been better able to help Daniel confront racism. The fact that she lives in an area where there is little direct racism means that, on the few occasions when she and Daniel have experienced such incidents, 'my breath has been taken away so entirely that I have dissolved into speechlessness. One of the earliest incidents was when Daniel was in a pushchair, hardly more than a baby. Waiting for a tube train, a young couple with two small children walked past us, obviously disapproving, along the empty platform. The little girl, about 4 years old, detached herself, ran back and sang "Nig, nog, sitting on a log", then "Ugh! He's got brown feet". I was speechless, looking at my beautiful baby, my mind reeling with feelings of distaste and sadness for the child.'

Heterosexism

Prejudice against lesbians starts in the school playground, as Kate's daughters found. She writes, 'My sexuality was initially quite difficult for my daughters to come to terms with, not because they minded, but they thought other people would . . . At school, they began to experience the usual run of anti-lesbian and anti-gay jokes and jibes on a personal level. My elder daughter felt totally unable to tackle them, because she feared persecution that she would not be able to deal with. My younger daughter could not associate me, or other lesbians she had come to know and like, with the hatred and dismissal of lesbians she encountered at school and play.'

Barbara Walker, whose son is 4, is aware that 'despite all I can do, it is inevitable that one day he will meet up with some of society's censorious attitudes to homosexuality. Our local council decided last year to encourage gay men and lesbians to come forward as possible foster parents but met with vociferous minority opposition. One Tory Councillor declared "I am not prepared to deliver the children of this borough in to the hands of filthy perverts". I hope that Tom will not be hurt or divided by such attitudes.'

As a single woman, Jean Walk has experienced hostility which, at times, has amounted to harassment. She writes, 'Almost all the women I know are married and when we go out together I find that their husbands think that I'm encouraging the women to go out without them.' One such man shouted at her, 'Just because you haven't got a man to come home to' and another came banging on her door, and threatened to hit her, accusing her of being to blame because his wife had been out late. Like Jean, Vivette Ferguson has had the word lesbian flung at her as a term of abuse. In Vivette's experience, it was her ex-boyfriend. He also tried to rape her when he found that she was sharing her flat with a woman friend: 'I don't think he knew how strong I was. I kneed him in the groin and chucked him out – which I feel very good about.'

Men as fathers

Women become single parents as a result of a number of different circumstances. Some of us explicitly chose to have a child on our own while others found that the relationship with our child(ren)'s father broke down at different stages – some at the very beginning of the pregnancy, some when children were very young, others much later. There are similarly a wide range of experiences in terms of both our own and our children's relationship with their father.

Some women feel a sense of betrayal in relation to their children's father. For Jean Walk and Vivette Ferguson, this sense of betrayal stems from behaviour which they felt was not compatible with family life. Jean writes of how she 'didn't want to be just a woman that's there to bring children into the world, to cook meals to put on the table when the man comes home from work, to sit indoors while he goes out . . . What I wanted out of life and out of a relationship was a partner. I wanted to be friends, to have a man as a companion.' After years of putting up with a man who was neither a companion nor a friend, Jean found she no longer loved him. Vivette also found that her love for her children's father faded after years of putting up with his behaving as if he were 'a single person, a man about town'. She wrote about how he was not really interested in caring for his children. 'He liked showing [Daniel] off, once he was clean and dressed. He would walk down the road exhibiting his wonderful son but he was never the sort of father who would take him off to a museum or the park for the afternoon.'

A strong feeling of betrayal does not sit easy with enabling a child to maintain a relationship with her/his father and Sheela Bonarjee makes no bones about her hatred for the man who not only abandoned his children but also stole her savings. 'I was so hurt that I broke off every possible connection with my husband and his family and I determined that he would never see his children again . . . When [the children] asked me about their father I told them the truth and I thoroughly poisoned their minds . . . I told them that if a father could cut his children off at such a young age, then he wasn't worth knowing.'

Neither Sheela's nor Vivette's children have any contact with their father and they do not feel that this has had any significant adverse effect on their children. Some mothers feel differently. For example, Carole Sturdy writes of her regret about the effect on her son of his father's absence. 'I have moments of really painful regret for the fact that Ciaran hasn't got a father who is around more often and who is more of a real presence in his life . . . He sometimes speaks in a wistfully envious way of boys who talk about things they've done with their dads at the weekend. And when we watch

TV programmes about families he sometimes says that he wishes he had a dad like that.' Jean Ellis recognises that her son will 'always carry a deep layer of sadness in him for the father he could not be with'. Each time Pierre-Marie has visited this country, Daniel has been plunged 'into a special sort of happiness and a terrible misery. I try to tell him that sadness is not always to be spurned. We must take it and make it part of our lives, and that maybe the time for them both is later, when Daniel is older. But although we do talk about it, there has been a part of Daniel which I barely reach, a private part of him'.

Fathers can play an important role even when there is conflict involved between the two parents. Pippa Murray recognises that her daughter, Jessie, 'has always been very attached to her father. She thoroughly enjoys the time she spends with him and misses him greatly.' I also wrote about how my daughter's father 'is a permanent and secure fixture in her life and she loves him very much. She has no concept of his being separated from her and her life.'

Relationships

Some women who spend time parenting on their own then move into other relationships, and sometimes marriage, which means that they are no longer single parents. By the nature of this book, none of the contributors had formed other relationships which changed their status as single parents. Some of us had tried having sexual relationships and sometimes these relationships seemed in conflict with our role as mothers. Eileen Phillips asked herself a number of questions when she embarked on a new relationship while her daughter was very young – 'I knew I didn't want a replacement daddy for Ella. Neither had I sorted out what my own needs were. Did I want a sexual relationship which would help me remember the pre-Ella me? Something that could contrast with the serious, committed responsible person who was setting about bringing up a child? Or was I on the search for stability and security – somebody who could lift some of the burden off my shoulders? I remember thinking then and later that sex was the only thing I might do which was of no benefit to Ella. Everything else in my life was geared towards her and the wish to make her happy and healthy. The sexual me was the only half which had no direct significance for her.'

Carole Sturdy felt that her sexual relationships could be positively damaging for her son, particularly when one man with whom she was involved started to assume the role of Ciaran's father. 'Although I cannot remember the details of this clearly now, I do remember Ciaran's distress and indignation, his insistence that Rik was his only real father, and my own failure to intervene . . . It gave me a glimpse of the awful possibilities of the scenario that appears in some child abuse cases; of the needy, single mother and equally needy, but violent, stepfather. I found I wasn't so very far from all that myself.'

A number of the contributors have written about the experience of being alone. Vivette Ferguson, for example, wrote, 'I have been celibate now for seven years. When Bernie left I wanted time on my own. I had feelings of failure as a mother, as a lover, as a person. I had made him leave but essentially he had rejected me. I needed time to get back my own self-esteem. I think you give up part of yourself when you enter into a relationship and I needed to get myself back. Having got myself back I'm not sure I ever want to give it to anyone else. It would be nice to have a relationship but I don't ever want to give my whole body and soul to anyone else again. The experience of being rejected meant that I spent some time getting back my confidence and self esteem and now I feel a whole person on my own.'

Families

Our own parents can have an important influence on the experience of single motherhood, particularly for women who become pregnant when they are still living with their parents. When Diana Richard's father finally found out that his 16-year-old daughter was pregnant, he stopped speaking to her – 'So far as he was concerned it was an embarrassment because I was so young and it was a reflection on him. It meant that he couldn't control his kids.' Angela Jules was also living with her parents when she became pregnant but, although her father never spoke to her about her pregnancy, she assumed he was supportive of her particularly as he paid for the cost of her daughter's christening. Like Diana's mother, her mother seemed to know her daughter was pregnant before being told. Angela writes, 'When I told my mother she said, "Yes, I know." She didn't mind that I was pregnant as I was by then a qualified secretary (which had been her ambition for me) and, as she said, I could always go back to work afterwards.'

Both Angela and Diana relied on their families for childcare to enable them to earn a living after their children were born. When Diana went to America to try to make a career for herself, her parents and sister looked after her son. However, when she came back to this country and lived again with her parents, she found that her role as Michael's mother had been eroded. 'My parents treated me like a teenage daughter, complaining about things like making a mess, not doing the washing up and so on. But I am also the mother of a child. I am not Michael's big sister. However, if I wanted to go out I had to ask my mother to babysit so I was still dependent on her . . . A neighbour said to me once "I see your sister is still playing mother to your child". That hurt. Especially as my mother's comment was that my sister was a better mother to Michael than I was.'

Legacies of childhood

Diana is aware that patterns experienced in her childhood are to some extent being repeated in her son's childhood. As the eldest child, she writes of how she had felt left out. 'My brothers and sisters all came one after another, taking my place, and I felt my mother didn't have time for me because she was so busy. I was closer to my aunt and my grandmother, particularly from the age of about nine when I started spending a lot of holidays with my grandmother. And, in a way, history is repeating itself because Michael spends so much time with his grandmother and aunt.'

Many of us are conscious of the legacies of our own childhood which we bring to our experiences of parenting. Jean Ellis' experience of separation from her mother accounts, she thinks, for her reluctance to parent in a couple relationship. She writes, 'I had spent my 20s recovering from what I had experienced as a very difficult and painful childhood. I had been at boarding-school since I was 7, my parents having divorced when I was a toddler. My own mother was a stranger to me, and, although my stepmother is a warm, caring person, I always felt on the periphery of the family groups I was supposedly part of. Families and I did not feel comfortable together.' At the same time, her own feelings about her mother – 'As a child myself I had desperately wanted my mother' – informed her recognition of her son's grief about his separation from his father.

Some of us who have had unhappy experiences in childhood found that becoming a parent reconciled us to the legacies of such a childhood. I wrote of the way that, 'The experience grounded me emotionally, reconciled me to my own childhood and enabled me to love and be loved in a way which healed the scars of my own insecurity and neediness . . . I had always assumed that I would love this child, completely and utterly, but I was not prepared for the way that she would completely and utterly love me. It had never occurred to me to expect reciprocated love'.

Separating

Part of the way in which becoming a mother can be a maturing process is the way our children become people separate from us as they grow older. The early recognition that a child is going to grow away from us can bring both grief and joy. Eileen Phillips writes of her conflicting feelings on the day her daughter started school. 'It was so contradictory. There I had been, keen for her to grow and develop, always encouraging her independence, knowing that I needed more space for myself and then suddenly, bam, totally distraught because she would have her own life now and not be my baby . . . Perhaps school is the first intimation that one day they will leave home and make their own way. It seems very important to know that is the future.'

Kate Mariat's future, now that her daughters are 19 and 16, will be structured by what she has discovered she wants for herself. In writing about her experience as a mother she has realised 'how autonomous we've each become. I'm no longer bound by the umbilical cord of their need for support – my need to give it. I no longer feel indispensable. I don't worry about them as much as I used to. I have confidence in their growing ability to make their own lives. In less than two years my younger daughter will be leaving home and my life will be truly my own.'

For someone like Pippa, however, whose son has learning difficulties and epilepsy, such a development cannot be taken for granted. 'I think about the future in a different way from my friends who have children with no disabilities. I cannot take any independence, once the children have grown up, for granted, as most parents do. It seems extremely unlikely that Kim will ever be completely independent.' And for Sheela, her adult children's independence brings mixed feelings. 'As for being alone,' she writes, 'I've enjoyed it over the last twenty years, but I think I'm going to enjoy it less as my children leave to start their own lives. It would have been nice to have had a partner to fall back on at this point, but I am thankful for the loyal friendship of my children.'

A stage in our lives

For most of us, the experience of being a single mother will be but one stage in our lives. Once our children are grown we will be single people again and indeed some of us see ourselves as single people now. The assumptions about what it means to be a single mother are not helpful to us and we often find it difficult to relate to such stereotypes. As Sindhu Hope wrote, 'My first thought when faced with writing about single parenthood was that I am not a real single parent. I realised that I carry an unconscious image of what constitutes a single parent. Poverty, youth, bad housing, no support network, shabby, sad, stressed and depressed. I surprise myself!' Like many of us, Angela Jules resists the labels applied to us – 'I feel that single mothers should not feel downhearted or alone. We should enjoy our children. The stigma of being unmarried is just a label and I don't feel all the negative things that are assumed to be part of being a single mother apply to me.'

Micheline Mason, in common with most of us, feels very positive about being a mother – 'I know that for Lucy and me, being a single-parent family works well'. She goes on to say that she has 'never lost sight of the fact that the main thing about becoming a parent, under any circumstances, is that you get to give life to a new, unique, priceless human being. In a society which really valued young people, parents would . . . be given every assistance necessary to do a good job despite any unfavourable circumstances. Single parents would not be seen as deviants, failures or social problems, but as people to be cherished and supported as life-givers, not resource-takers.'

This book is about real lives: women's experiences and concerns as single parents are presented in our own terms. The contributions cover a diverse and complex reality yet there are also common themes. I hope that the book will go some way towards creating a compassionate understanding of what it is like to be a single mother, an understanding which incorporates both the wonderful and the difficult things about the experience.

BEYOND ANGER

SHEELA BONARJEE

I had no idea that he was having an affair but in fact it had been going on for two years. During the first ten years of our marriage we were happy and had a very good social life. Lots of parties and 'Beautiful People'. When I had the children, he started to feel tied down. He became more and more disgruntled about not having the social life he had enjoyed, about the misery of having children, what a mistake it had been. He said we should never have embarked on this and that I had wanted the children while he hadn't – although in fact it had been a joint decision. Gradually I realised that he was opting out of the marriage.

Then one day, just by chance, I discovered that when he said he would be away on business he was in fact not. So when he got home from work I said let's discuss it; you are having an affair. He said who told you? I told him that he had to make up his mind – either you are a husband and family man or you carry on your bachelor life. You can't have both. I am a 100 per center. If I do something, I put my whole heart into it. When he said he couldn't give her up, I told him, 'if that's the line you take then you can't have both, you can't have her *and* the home and the children'. He left. He then went off to Nigeria with the woman with whom he had been having an affair.

He not only rejected me, he rejected his children. They were only 4 and 2 years old. I was so bitter that I didn't allow him to see them again.

How it all began

In 1953 I left my home in a small hill station in the Himălaya mountains. I came to England from India to continue my education. I was then 19. I met my ex-husband soon after. He was writing an MA thesis on Asians in East Africa and did most of his research at the India Office library. The Europeans I had met in India were not interested in Indians so I was intrigued by his enthusiasm for the subject. Within a year of meeting we got married. He didn't tell me then that he had been married before.

After my marriage in 1957 I started a business, housing students and visitors to London. I myself had found it difficult to get accommodation as the English landlady at that time openly advertised 'No Coloureds, No Cats and No Children'. I became the first Black woman to run an accommodation agency, I worked with the University Lodging Bureau, Citizens' Advice Bureaux and various embassies. At that time, many African and Asian Embassies were setting up their offices in London and I was recommended by the British Council as the person to whom they should come to find accommodation for their staff. I in turn would go to landlords and landladies in Kensington, Westminister, Hampstead, Chelsea and ask them for properties for Black professionals. I came across a lot of prejudice. Landlords had no qualms about saying whom they didn't want – they would tell me 'We don't like Jews, Irish or Coloured people'.

From this experience I vowed that I would never be in a situation where I was dependent on someone else's prejudices. I would buy my own house and educate my children in private schools in order to protect them from racism.

I ran my housing agency for eight years and then, when my daughter was born in 1965, I sold the business for £10,000. I thought that the money was for my children's future, to use to protect them against the prejudices that they would inevitably come up against.

My son was born in 1967. I settled down to the life of a mother and housewife and was so busy with the children that my husband took over responsibility for investing my money. I had wanted to invest my money in property but he said it would be better putting the money into shares. He said I would never have the time to organise the lettings, with two children to look after. I didn't understand shares but he did and he made quite a lot of money; he bought shares in the Beatles before they became famous and sold them profitably. He made many other good investments. Initially, we bought shares in our joint names and when he came to sell them I would sign whatever was necessary. However, later and unknown to me, when it came to buying shares the next time round he bought them in his name only. I was so engrossed with the children that I didn't realise he hadn't asked me to sign anything for a long time. He went on buying and selling in his own right. When he left he took all the money which was by then invested in shares only in his name.

Soon after he left I went to our bank and asked to see our joint accounts. I had been with Barclays Bank in Mayfair since the days of running my business there. The manager knew that I had sold the business and invested the money through the bank. He showed me the current account but when I asked to see the share accounts he said he couldn't show them to me because they were not in my name. 'It's not your account,' he said. He told me that he couldn't tell me anything about the shares because they were solely in my husband's name. My husband left for Nigeria, and took all the money.

When I found out I was so hurt that I broke off every possible connection with my husband and his family and I determined that he would never see his children again. I decided that the children would be entirely my commitment. I didn't want our lives divided and undermined with him coming, bringing presents and dividing my children's loyalties. I was determined that I would see them through. I knew it would destroy me if he came with bribes for the children.

I doubt if he cared that much as he had gone off to Nigeria. I don't think I am a praiseworthy person either. I did my best to deprive him of his children. These days people are supposed to be civilised about divorce and remain friends. I could not. I feel I am not very civilised. I had so much venom and hatred towards him. He took the money and he left the children unprovided for. After thirteen years of marriage I thought that was a terrible thing to do. I felt betrayed and cheated.

Now, looking back, I suppose he was an immature man. He was an only child of parents who did nothing but dote on him. We had a good marriage for ten years, that is, before the two children arrived. We were both earning good salaries but when I sold the business we lost half our income. The children took my attention and he felt left out. He was unable to cope with that. If somehow I had been able to hold on to him, I think maybe we could have made it work. But he had not got the maturity and I may have been too rigid in my attitude by expecting him to become wholeheartedly a family man. But at the time, I thought to hang on to him would destroy me. If something doesn't work, then it doesn't work and you just have to cut it out. If he didn't want children then I had to take the responsibility for them alone.

After he left

I had no job, my savings had gone and I had a mortgage of £6,500 – a lot of money in those days. I let out every room in the house, keeping only one room for myself and the children. I got myself into the London School of Economics, completed a degree and later got a job as a lecturer.

It was hard being a single parent. One night I came back from the LSE when the clocks had just gone back, and it suddenly gets dark. The children were used to my getting home at a certain time but when I got in that night they were sitting in the hall by the door crying their eyes out. The person who had been looking after them said she had been trying to tell them it was all right even if it was dark but they were convinced that I had left them. When I came in they said, 'Oh Mummy, we thought you had died or gone away.' I took them into our room and I got into bed with both of them and said, 'I will never leave you.' I held them and said 'You are like my arms and my legs to me, would I cut them off? Don't you know that you are from my body? You are part of me. I could never cut my children off. I will never, ever leave you.' I think that it gave them strength to know that even if they had only one parent, they had a truly committed parent.

We were together a lot while they were children, my holidays as a teacher coinciding with theirs. We went away together, we went on day trips, on holidays with my family in France. We did a lot of things together.

When they asked me about their father I told them the truth and I thoroughly poisoned their minds. I told them that I had saved a large sum of money and that it was for their education. I told them that we would not have been poor if we had had that money. I told them that he had taken from them what I had put aside for their future. I told them that if a father could cut his children off at such a young age, then he wasn't worth knowing.

They didn't contest this. But later on my son, when he was going through the problems of a teenager, would say to me, 'I'm going to go to my father.' I would tell him that he could; he could find his father through his grandparents. However, he was only using it as a weapon. He soon stopped saying things like that once he became aware that I called his bluff. He has since grown up into a kind and responsible young man and has never made any attempt to contact his father.

My daughter has never bothered about her father, although in fact she has some memory of him. Like her brother she has made no attempt to contact him. And neither has their father made any attempt to contact his children.

Protecting my children against racism

I was very conscious of prejudice both as an Asian and as a single parent. When my children were in a state primary school I became chairperson of the PTA, only because I wanted to know exactly what was going on in the school and to try to protect my children from prejudice. As chairperson of the PTA, there was no point in my name being Bonarjee and their's being Lycett (my ex-husband's name). So through most of their school life they were called Bonarjee. However, when my daughter came to take her GCEs, her first public exams, I told her she had to take those exams in the name of Lycett. I insisted on this because I was afraid of prejudice. Why should my children bear a cross that they don't have to bear? Neither of the children look particularly Asian, so having the name Bonarjee was what really identified them as Asian. Once they were Lycett, their Asian origins were not apparent.

My daughter's GCEs were the beginning of her going out into the world, going through university and getting jobs and therefore I felt she needed to have her qualifications in the name of Lycett. She put up a big fight and said she wouldn't take this name. But I insisted and so she took both her O and A levels using her name Lycett. She then went through university as Lycett, doing a post-graduate degree in Languages. Now she's working in a good job and I don't think she would go back to using Bonarjee.

My son was more willing to take on the name Lycett because he suffered more prejudice in school. I think being a boy he was more exposed. He took a degree in computing. I am sure he would not have got that job in the company he is in if he had applied under the name Bonarjee.

I feel it's sad that they haven't got my name but I just didn't want them to bear an unnecessary cross. I'm not fighting great causes, I'm protecting them so that they can make a better life. The fact that I need to do this says something about this society but then all societies are racist. I'm old enough to see the prejudice in Indian society with its castes, its creeds, its intolerance. I feel we live in an unfair and unjust world and we have to wear the gloves for it.

And what about me?

People said that I myself would have done better if I had kept the name Lycett; all this nonsense about being able to pass as white. But I felt I had to go back to my own name. I felt such hate for the man that I could not carry his name.

I was very conscious of prejudice against me as a single mother. When I first applied for a teaching job, one of the interview panel apparently expressed reservations about whether I could do the job as a single parent. Luckily the Principal of the College – a woman who had herself been a single mother – stood up for me and said that had nothing to do with the appointment of a candidate. This was in 1974 and that was quite a strong position to take then, so I was very lucky. However, my career *has* suffered as a result of being a single parent. I couldn't go to evening meetings, stay late at work and so on. The day I was appointed to my current job, seventeen years ago, three men were also appointed as lecturers and I've seen all of them move up the career ladder whereas I have not. It's nothing to do with my competence because I'm a good teacher. I have just never had the time to get involved with all the manoeuvring that goes on in the department. Now it's too late, I'm 57 and I am taking early retirement. I do feel some regret. These three men now hold very senior positions. They have had careers *and* families. It would have been nice for me to be able to retire at a higher level, with a better pension.

It's been very difficult to have relationships with men without being divided, torn apart between a man and my children. I *have* had relationships but it has been so traumatic that in the end it hasn't been worth the pain. When men come and then they go, the children think, as my son once expressed, that they have been betrayed again.

I know I've done the best thing for my children. But for me, when I retire my pension will be fairly small. However, given the chance, I wouldn't do things differently. As for being alone, I've enjoyed it over the last twenty years, but I think I'm going to enjoy it less as my children leave to start their own lives. It would have been nice to have had a partner to fall back on at this point, but I am thankful for the loyal friendship of my children.

As for . . .

If I saw my children's father now I would like to say to him that it all turned out very well, in spite of him. I'm proud of my children. As you sow, you reap. He has no children and to me he is the loser, especially now when I am just reaping all the joy of the past. I have a friendship with both my children. The bonding between the three of us is strong. They have known a strong, committed parent for whom they were always the first and the most important thing. You cannot give them anything better.

TO GREAT APPLAUSE

JEAN ELLIS

My son Daniel was born to great applause. Literally. He was born by vacuum extraction, a method which, so the doctor told me later, had not been used in Aberdeen Maternity Hospital for some time. In my groggy state at the end of a long labour, I was aware of an increasing number of white-coated figures crowding into the delivery room to watch the birth, then clapping as the baby arrived. Whether they were clapping my efforts, or those of the baby, the doctor, or the technology, I was never sure.

'He's got your chin,' one of them called out. Prominent, she meant. Determined, I thought. And I certainly had been determined to have my baby. Increasingly in my late-twenties I had felt compelled towards parenthood. I had reached the stage of seeing pregnant women and babies everywhere, and, without becoming obsessed, knew that I would have to take some practical steps towards having a baby. Although I wanted a child, I could never imagine myself living in any sort of 'traditional' family situation. I had been in relationships of various sorts and conditions in the past, but had always felt it unlikely that I would want or be able to live with a man for any great period of time. Certainly, I had never felt inclined to have a family with any of the men I had been involved with. There seemed to be a sort of unformulated test which they failed to pass.

I had spent my twenties recovering from what I had experienced as a very difficult and painful childhood. I had been at boarding-school since I was 7, my parents having divorced when I was a toddler. My own mother was a stranger to me, and, although my stepmother is a warm, caring person, I always felt on the periphery of the family groups I was supposedly part of. Families and I did not feel comfortable together.

So by the time I was 28 I was on my way to work in Cameroon in West Africa for two years, thinking of babies, and wondering whether I could adopt on my return. As it happened, within weeks I fell into a very deep relationship. Pierre-Marie, the man who was to be Daniel's father, was the first man who I had never wanted or tried to change, despite any number of imperfections, and I suppose that might have been the test other men had failed. Anyway, we decided almost straightaway to have a child together and never thought afterwards about reconsidering the idea. At the same time, it was always understood, although never clearly stated, that I would not stay in Cameroon, but would return once my contract was over to have the baby in England, on my own. On my side I am not sure how far this decision stemmed from my distrust in my ability to live with anyone at all, and how much from my belief that I would be engulfed by Cameroonian social constraints once I was no longer protected by the status of my job and became a mere mother. More contradictory, there were characteristics which this man had which attracted me madly, a certain arrogance, for example, which at the same time I knew I could never live with.

As my two-year job contract drew to a close, we crossed our fingers and tried for the baby. Incredibly, I became pregnant within three months, and was able to stay on in the country for another five months in a state of high excitement and trepidation, before returning to England, mentally clutching to me my barely swollen belly, and my closely guarded secret.

It had never occurred to me to worry about the reactions of my family in Scotland. This was partly because my relationship with my parents did not include looking for approval or agreement. But more than that, becoming pregnant was one of the few things I had ever done in which I had been driven by complete certainty that it was the only choice I had to make. Thinking about it now, I realise that this was a delusion. There were other options. Anyway, it seemed to be my concern, not anyone else's. Undoubtedly there was some disappointment in my family about my news. I had written a letter telling them about my pregnancy just before leaving Cameroon, far too late for discussion to change anything. I am under the impression that my younger sisters felt that I had let them down – that I had been set on the route for an exciting career, a free spirit, untrammelled by family ties, but now doomed to sink under a layer of nappies. On the other hand, perhaps that is a projection of my own feelings. Maybe it was not them, but another part of me which felt let down. Yet, at the time, I had no thoughts but that life would continue much as before – and that I would look for my next job in Paris, or Geneva, baby on back. Nappies never entered my fantasy. Cloud-cuckoo-land indeed!

There was a price to pay for feeling that the whole baby business was so entirely my own affair. Other people believed me, or had arrived at that view independently. I had imagined in the unformulated way that characterised all my preconceptions about motherhood, that friends, and, even more so, members of my family, would come rushing around to help. This would surely be a natural reaction given that I was on my own. Nothing could have been further from the truth, particularly in the early years. My last months of pregnancy and the actual childbirth were extraordinarily lonely days. I had found a new job in London and borrowed a friend's flat while she was away overseas. I spent my evenings alone, writing letters to Cameroon, eating Caribbean ginger cake and ice cream, and putting on an enormous amount of weight in a ridiculously short period of time. Until eventually, less than a week before the birth, with soaring blood pressure, and frantically reading up books on correct breathing during labour, I boarded the train to Aberdeen and my parents' warm house, with instructions to the train guard about the hospitals to contact *en route* should the baby show signs of arriving. I should add that my medical preparations for the birth had been perfunctory, to say the least, the result of returning from overseas so late in the day. No natural childbirth classes for me!

Contradictions

Daniel was born shortly before Christmas, with all the colour and activity around, a lovely time to be born. The combination of distance from, and closeness to, my family was reflected in my mixed feelings about having my baby in my parents' house. If they were not demonstrably enthusiastic about the baby, at least they had never asked any questions, and that seemed a good enough beginning. And they gave practical support at that time, which was more than a beginning. When I brought Daniel from the hospital we slept together in the spare attic bedroom, and for three weeks I made a regular nest of it, having nothing to do except care for my baby, while my stepmother, bless her, cooked and cared for me. It was probably the happiest time of my life. My hopes for the future were boundless, and despite the endless messages I recorded to Peirre-Marie on cassettes which were never posted, I felt supremely self-sufficient, able to indulge a selfishness in relation to my baby which those who have to share can never do. He was all mine. But it was a short-lived idyll. My maternity leave was six weeks only, and we were soon back to our short-life accommodation in London, two tiny rooms in a shared house, and my new job, interesting, but part-time and badly paid. I had joined a housing co-operative in the month before Daniel was born. It was set up to cater for the needs of single parents in particular, with an active culture of childcare support between co-op members, and with the hope of a brand new flat in a few years. I am still surprised at how quickly I had chosen a lifestyle which gave me maximum time with the baby, and how soon the notion of continental jobs and nannies and continued travel disappeared. I sometimes wonder where that other path might have led. Meanwhile my reality was running the gauntlet of cold rooms, damp and peeling walls, with a bathroom too unhealthy to be used for the baby, and co-op committee meetings in smoke-filled rooms, many of us holding crying babies on our knees.

I was lucky enough to be able to take Daniel into work for the first few months. At the time the organisation I was working with had no recognisable management structure and was women-dominated. To my colleagues, a black baby in the office, and a single mum to whom they paid nanny expenses while she went on field trips to Mauritania, was added proof of their radical intent and fitted their image. To them it was an exciting experiment. We want to see if it works, if we can do it as well, they said in my interview, barely asking me about my credentials.

That first year was in fact wholly exhilarating. The organisation of babysitting with other single parents in the housing co-op more or less worked, enabling even the occasional evening out, and, indeed later, regular evening classes. I frequently spent weekends working as a committee member for other organisations. Daniel was a regular visitor to crèches, and benefited from those early days of concern for equal opportunities in the voluntary sector, when no meeting could be arranged without a crèche worker. I made my first field trip to Mauritania when Daniel was four months old, leaving him to the care of a wonderful agency nanny. Wandering alone along the beach at Dakar while waiting for planes, or feeling my brain slowly moving into gear as I read international news magazines in hotel rooms, or sat around with villagers along the Senegal River discussing the ploughing season, I really believed I had pulled it off, that I could have it all – my cake, the icing, and the whole lot.

The danger signals were there, of course, and it had never been plain sailing. For a start, taking Daniel into work was a brilliant idea in principle, but rocking a new born baby to sleep while phoning, or doing accounts, and breastfeeding during meetings, were never a lot of fun. Finding a child-minder when the experiment turned sour for my colleagues and they shouted enough, proved to be a nightmare, although we were lucky in the end. Then my times away, although not frequent, did cause problems. Daniel was basically a blissfully easy baby, but after my overseas trips, he would refuse to sleep at night unless I was holding him, then the nights became hopelessly broken, and I began to tip into perpetual fatigue.

The truth was that during the first few years of Daniel's life I was experiencing two very different underlying sets of emotions. There was the feeling of self-sufficiency and sheer contentedness at being alone with my child, of being the sole decision-maker, and the exhilaration of succeeding at what I had set out to do. At the same time, for the first time ever I had become fearful. My student days had also been spent in London, and then I would without a thought walk back to digs miles across London in the middle of the night. Now I held my breath in near terror as I walked back from the underground in the dark, particularly when Daniel was with me, sleeping in his sling. I had even become scared to cross the road without looking in all directions several times, and once had become almost hysterical when I fell with the baby on an icy road, convinced that I had cracked his head.

These fears had started as soon as Daniel was born. Perhaps it was a form of post-natal depression, but then I had felt wonderful so long as I was holding him. The terrible anxieties started in hospital whenever he was taken back to the nursery. I was the only one on the ward who could not sleep at night, and I would haunt the corridor outside the nursery, peering in at the little bundles to get a glimpse of mine. As I was also the only one breast feeding, sometimes the nurses would let me into the nursery at night after I had fed him. This calmed my anxieties somewhat, but back in bed I had dreadful fits of weeping at the sudden responsibility. It was not the being alone, but the shock of loving so suddenly and so unreservedly which had shaken me. I realised with complete clarity that I would never be free again. Not only were my own needs now subjected to the overriding desire for the very best for my child, but I felt overwhelmed by the vision of a lifetime of fear for his physical safety. The fact that my happiness was now tied in with another person's existence was wholly terrifying. I am certain that the feeling of being alone in facing that responsibility heightened my fears, although I know now that these are familiar enough fears for new parents. But at the time I was certainly the only mother in the ward crying, and the hospital staff treated me as though it were wholly unacceptable.

The same feeling of intense vulnerability, which had gripped me in that hospital ward, hit me again over the next few years. The house I lived in was surrounded by empty houses, and I was terrified that our flat would be broken into. Even after I had fixed bars to the windows, not only did I not go to bed until the pubs were closed, but I would not put the lights out until the streets were silent. Perhaps the fears were not entirely without good reason, but my waking nightmares went further. They were of murder and rape and babies smashed against walls.

So that was the most striking contradiction in those early days. In many ways I felt strong emotionally, more so than I had ever been. Finally adult, I had enormous faith in myself as a parent, powerful in the organisation of my life and my work. Yet at the same time I felt physically weak, vulnerable, exposed, and craved protection.

As Daniel grew older the pendulum swung in the opposite direction. My fears faded, but the euphoria and enormous energy which had carried me through the first two years also began to fade. The travelling part of my job became increasingly difficult. I came to dread field trips, and sometimes two weeks before I left I still did not know who would be looking after Daniel while I was away. Retrospectively, I have no reason to believe that my absences had a long-term harmful effect on Daniel. He was always a cheerful and secure little boy, and his life in the housing co-op, going to a childminder and later a day nursery meant that he was happy to mix with anyone, and went self-assured into any situation. But when he was nearly 3, he reacted badly after one trip. Never an agressive child, he kicked out at me for a few weeks after my return, so I knew the time had come to find a new job.

The next stage

The price of finding work with no travelling was moving into a full-time job, with a heavy schedule of evening meetings. It was a mistake, but I still believed at that time that almost everything was possible. Life soon turned into an endless round of childcare arrangements, rushed meals and meetings – evening meetings for work, weekend meetings for the co-op. It was a new phase of our lives, particularly as, when Daniel was 3, I met Mike. He shared the care of his 2 year old daughter, Jessie, with his ex-partner, and it looked as if I had found what was for me the ideal family: non-conforming and non-nuclear.

However, the exhausting routine of a new relationship, energy put into two children and a demanding job, combined with moving house, resulted in my developing glandular fever and having a near physical collapse. I left work and have been self-employed since then, often working part-time to allow for school holidays. In many ways that decision marked the collapse in my belief that I could continue in the same direction as I had been heading before the baby days. When I developed glandular fever, any remaining energy I had evaporated, and my new relationship, after the honeymoon period was over, brought with it new levels of depression. One of the problems was the unresolved nature of the type of family unit we were. This not quite nuclear family had its difficulties. Its very ambiguities carried not the freedom I imagined, but some very destructive elements. Although living together, we never operated as a single unit. My partner expected me to relate to him with the emotional responses of a single person while financially, morally and physically I remained solely responsible for my son. I also took the main responsibility for the domestic life of the whole household. This was a no-win situation and I knew it, although it took a long time before I accepted the inevitable conclusions. Despite the fact that our love for each other's children grew with the years, the damage done to our feelings for each other was too great, and after six years we separated.

Perhaps because the relationship between Daniel and me is so strong, to outsiders our connection with Mike and Jessie appeared to be inconsequential. Maybe they did not see how we could exist both as a single-parent family and as part of a larger family unit at the same time, and how painful it was for us to lose a partner and a daughter, a father and a sister. Of all the lack of support we have had, the total absence of support we had at that time has been the hardest for me to understand and bear.

So, we had a six-year interlude to being totally on our own, and in that way I was able to see the benefits of being in a larger unit – the family holidays, picnics in the summer and the joy of being able to spread one's affections more widely, to avoid the tendency to suffocate in the one-to-one intense, loving relationship. On the other hand, the advantages of being on our own again soon became clear. Daniel and I became as close as we had been when he was small. He picked up my thoughts to the extent that often I stopped myself from passing a remark because it was inevitable that within thirty seconds he would say it for me. I could now take Daniel to his music and dance classes without having to take into account the need to cook dinner for anyone else. I did not have to justify my willingness to spend five hours out of the house on a Monday evening on these activities, or the time we spent sitting together at the piano. Perhaps more importantly, there was no longer the anger and exhaustion, which had found expression in my shouting at Daniel, and our house generally became the calmer place it had been in his baby days.

One thing my relationship with Mike, or rather with his daughter, Jessie, had shown me was the negative side of my feelings for my son. I recognised that, to a great extent, the way I loved Jessie was healthier. I did not want anything for her but for her to be herself. She was not part of my fight against my own childhood ghosts. Also from that childhood I had a role model of what it was to be a good stepmother, but not one for a mother. While wanting the best for Jessie, as I did for Daniel, I felt no need for her to do, or to be, or to achieve anything in particular. Unburdened by expectations, our relationship gave little houseroom to pressures, or disappointments, or anger or any other projection of the problems which we foist on our own children. I can barely remember a time when I felt angry with her. Whereas with Daniel, although intellectually I knew all the dangers, I wanted everything for him, all the things which I had wanted for myself but had not had. He was so desperately part of me, so unseparated. As deep were the feelings of love I had for him, as intense was the anger which I directed at him from time to time.

Separating

My son has just turned 12 now. I am conscious of our need to separate gradually and hope my awareness will help us to do that. More and more his music and dancing and other interests are activities which he pursues without me. But otherwise Daniel shows no great signs of pulling away, although he has a strong mind of his own, and I suspect is doing it by stealth, and I will be shocked one day to find how much his own person he has become. That is how he is. For me, my need to know the everyday details of Daniel's life, to share his successes and disappointments, is a hard one to to be weaned from.

Apart from being able to spend enormous amounts of time together doing things we enjoy, in more general terms, the advantage of being a single parent has been that I have not had to consult anybody at all. I have simply followed my instincts, recognising that they may sometimes be at fault, but I can live with that. For example, I have always been very strict, to such an extent that I am very much out of step with other parents. Bedtimes have always been rigorously kept to, with no excuses allowed, apart from illness, for getting out of bed again. There was virtually no snacking between meals, and food on the plate was there to be eaten. I wonder if I could ever have learnt to discuss or compromise on these issues with a second parent. I am glad that Daniel did not have to listen to two parents fighting over the right course of action. By and large he has accepted my rules without question. This has not made him docile or compliant because there have always been large areas of our joint lives which he could influence, certainly more so than if there had been a second adult around. In many ways he has taken the place of that second adult, more often than not being the decision-maker on what we should eat, or where we should go on holiday, or which show or film we should see. The basic structure of Daniel's everyday life, his bedtimes, meals, homework etc, is set by me, with his agreement; the rest he has maximum control over.

If I feel free to be more strict in my parenting than many might choose, I also feel free to be more physically close. We have always kissed and hugged more than I see others doing. He will still sometimes sit on my knee, and we usually watch television in a huddle. I often feel that my parents and friends have as many reservations about our physical closeness as they have about my strictness. However none has been so unwise as to voice their feelings in any overt way. Only twice, and that quite recently, has that happened, on the one hand because I was seen as being too hard, and in the second case because I was seen as being too soft. In both cases I was astonished at how angry I became. In the one instance I said: 'Don't tell me how to bring up my child. We have to live our lives together, so let us get on with it.' On the second occasion my response was similar. In this case it was my mother's husband whom I sat down with and talked vehemently to. He and my mother had not seen Daniel and me since Daniel was a toddler. I had raised Daniel on my own, I said, without any help from anyone, and *no one*, but *no one* had the right to pass judgement or to comment. In the calm I realise that perhaps all this self-reliance is not entirely a good thing, and that maybe we could have benefited from someone else's view or experience. The idea of going round to Mum's with the kids for a chat on a Saturday afternoon, which I pull out of my vision of other people's family life, is an attractive one. Contradictions again.

Daniel's father

Where does Daniel's father come into all this? To my surprise, he too, if he has any feelings about my choices for his son, holds his tongue. I believe this is also because he realises that the problems, the responsibilities, have all been mine. Yet I do feel that he has a right to express a preference, and I would listen, despite the fact that we have seen him so little.

Daniel is after all, *our* child, not just mine, and, so many years later, I realise how little Pierre-Marie and I explored how he would feel about the separation from Daniel and me. I never allowed myself to think about how unhappy Pierre-Marie was at my leaving the country pregnant. I know it now, although at the time he had sufficient pride and sheer obstinacy not to show whatever feelings he had. It was only back in London, during the last months of my pregnancy, that we both felt the loss, and an avalanche of letters flowed in both directions. After the birth I felt extraordinarily connected to him and sent photos of the baby every few weeks, and chronicled every little advance Daniel made during his baby months.

It was impossible not to talk to Daniel about his father, and his father must always have been part of his consciousness. Indeed, I had never believed that there was any option but that my child should know as much as possible about his father. As a child myself I had desperately wanted my own mother. I thought she was the most beautiful person in the world. I saw her for only one day a year, or less, a day to be waited for with a desperate longing and excitement.

Despite all that, I had never understood how our story would develop. For a start, I had an incredibly naïve vision of what our contact would be over the years. I thought Pierre-Marie and I would remain loving friends for life, having wonderful, romantic meetings at airports over the years, amplified by longer visits to Cameroon. I certainly had never imagined that I would have to face the reality of a low income, preventing us from finding the air fare to Cameroon, or that Pierre-Marie would marry and have another family which would absorb his energies. Or that having saved for the whole of Daniel's first year, our first holiday in Cameroon would be marred by a petty argument leading to bitterness which it would take years to overcome. Or, later, that I would resent being the one having to pay for the visits while it was Pierre-Marie's second family which had the deep freeze, the video and the rest. Away from Pierre-Marie I always feel warm, affectionate, accepting. I never expect more than he can give, a few letters a year. After all, as I have been reminded, that was the choice I made. But face to face with some of the issues, my feelings, forgotten so quickly, are real enough. In an entry in my diary while on holiday in Cameroon when Daniel was 8, I wrote:

> Daniel spent the night at Pierre-Marie's. Pierre Marie has just turned up with Daniel and Dominique [his second son]. He has left Dominique with me for the day, without giving me time even to protest, without thinking that I might have plans of my own, that I need a rest from childcare on my holiday. I want to shout at him: 'I have looked after your child for eight years by myself. I haven't come here to look after your other children as well.'

Ouch! There must be a few resentments lying fallow there. Strange that once back in London those feelings disappear. In fact I have always given Daniel a very positive image of his father. I was naïve then not to realise that he would adore both the idea of his father, and later the reality, and miss him dreadfully when he was not with him. The questions came as soon as Daniel started day nursery, despite the number of children there from single parent households. 'Where's *my* daddy?' At two years he would be pointing to black men passing in the street, saying 'Is that my daddy?' or climbing on the knee of any visitor to the house with the Cameroon photograph album, proudly showing the photos of 'my daddy'.

Yet Daniel was a happy child. The absence of his father only affected him in any noticeably painful way after they had met for the first time since he was a baby, when his father came to England on business when Daniel had just turned 8. It was an extraordinarily emotional time for all of us. We flung ourselves at each other in the foyer of a guest house in Bayswater. Father and son adored each other from the start, and I could not help sharing with Daniel some feelings of pride as we presented a unit for the first time since he was a baby. How does that square with my feelings of independence?

And then I had never anticipated the pain Daniel would go through as the day for leaving came closer. Half way through the visit he had started displaying disturbed behaviour, scratching and hitting himself, my son who had never had so much as a temper tantrum in his life. I knew I had to get him to understand his feelings, so Mike and I sat on either side of him and hugged him while he held himself rigid. I said, 'It's OK darling, you can cry, you can scream!' So he did. He just screamed and screamed while we held him, and I cried as well, both for him and for myself for the loss of my own mother. Daniel seemed to heal remarkably after that, but I knew that he had changed – that he would always carry a deep layer of sadness in him for the father he could not be with. And that is how it has been since. Pierre-Marie has returned twice since then, each time plunging Daniel into a special sort of happiness and a terrible misery. I try to tell him that sadness is not always to be spurned. We must take it and make it part of our lives, and that maybe the time for them both is later, when Daniel is older. But although we do talk about it, there has been a part of Daniel which I barely reach, a private part of him. Maybe I hold back, because of the fear that ours was a foolish, naïve venture which should not have been so lightly undertaken. Although I had never taken the view that the father could be cut out completely, I had miscalculated, whether through naïvety or sheer lack of imagination, how the situation would define and shape my child. Although I would back any woman's right to have a child on her own, I would now say don't make assumptions about what you child's needs will be.

Challenges

I had also failed to think through how, bringing up Daniel on my own, I would confront issues to do with gender and race, although I had recognised that these issues would be important. In fact, in order to bring up a boy to be gentle and caring, and in touch with his feelings, I felt his father's absence was almost essential, given his own stereotypical views of what constituted acceptable male behaviour. But on issues of race identity and raising my son to understand and face racism personally and politically, I had to regret that we were not together. Pierre-Marie is so strong and secure in his identity as an African. I would have liked Daniel to have been closer to that.

The assumptions in Cameroonian society about a woman's role in the family, and my own experience in relation to men while there, were undoubtedly among the reasons why I felt that I could not live in Cameroon on any sort of permanent basis. The basic attitudes in Britain and Cameroon are not so very different, but in Britain it is easier, at least at the personal level, to escape them to a degree. My feelings were reconfirmed by my first visit back to Cameroon when Daniel was a baby. On my only holiday since my pregnancy, I not only spent the entire time traipsing to the market and staggering back with food and bottles of beer for Pierre-Marie's friends to drink Daniel's health, cooking and cleaning in the heat and in conditions which had nothing to do with fitted kitchens or hoovers, but, even more infuriating, I was not allowed to discuss such things as financial matters. Not my concern, apparently, as if I had not managed my life entirely alone for the last year. Even Daniel, a 9 month old baby, was not allowed in the kitchen; it was no place for a boy, his father said.

So, raising Daniel alone, I was able to follow my convictions and my instincts about bringing up a son who was not only aware of gender inequalities but who would himself value women and girls in a way which remains unusual among young boys, and who would, I hoped, avoid some of the characteristics valued as appropriate male behaviour. One of Daniel's earliest toys which accompanied him everywhere was a small doll, but I was not overly concerned about toys. The exception was weapons, which were banned. I even took out the tiniest bullets, which came with space ships, and rendered them useless as fighting machines! Without guns, Daniel never rushed around play shooting or play fighting, and I always felt somewhat impatient with parents who claimed that even if they did not give their boys guns, they would use a stick or their fingers, to 'shoot' with. This simply did not happen in our experience. And for whatever reason, Daniel was never one to fall in a heap, tussling and fighting as much as his friends. I was also highly selective about programmes watched on television. There were never arguments; we simply did something else.

Daniel had a gentle nature from an early age, but I am sure it would have been easy not to have encouraged it, to have persuaded him into more generally acceptable male behaviour or pursuits. Although I think the messages surrounding children are important, for instance in books, or on the television, or given by the toys they play with, there seemed to me to be other more important influences, such as the time spent playing with children far younger than him, or the behaviour he was encouraged in or discouraged from when he was with Jessie. His music and dancing have also been important, bringing him continually into the company of girls and away from an endless round of football or skateboarding.

I never had any doubts about any of these things, and feel enormously proud of the person Daniel has become. Yet, as he has grown older, I have probably compromised more. He retreats into silence at times, behaviour I have found so difficult to accept in adult men. I hope I will come to terms with it, and whatever else emerges as he takes an ever-increasing role in shaping his own character. It will be a struggle for me, I am sure of that. I have accepted that there will be a compromise somewhere between my ideals and the reality presented by society as it is now, but I also wonder if I simply do not see the issues as clearly as I did when Daniel was younger. As I turn back to finding my own creativity and a new personal direction, perhaps I simply do not care as much.

I am not sure if this is true also in relation to my approach to bringing Daniel up as a black child. There are two strands to this issue. One is about his need to relate to his Cameroonian family and culture as well as to his white family, and the second concerns being black in a multi-racial society still dominated by white values and power structures. Through all that, the essential facts are that my black son lives with a white mother while his black father lives thousands of miles away. This is central to our existence as a family within society.

Keeping Daniel aware of and close to his Cameroonian roots has felt in some ways the easier of the two elements to deal with, particularly in the early days, when friends from Cameroon were perhaps around more than they are now. I was rigorous in cooking Cameroonian food, listening to Cameroonian music, going to cultural events, and Daniel has every book on Cameroon that I can find. There were more important things than this of course. I had always felt linked in many ways to Pierre-Marie's family when living in Cameroon. I was always happy to spend days in the family house in the village, allowing the conversation and family life to flow over me. I had promised Pierre-Marie's mother that I would bring her first grandchild to see her as soon as possible, and it was that which drove me back to Cameroon when Daniel was only 9 months old. Later, back in London, as I was dragging sodden nappies to the launderette, still without a car or a washing machine, I wondered if I was crazy to have spent my money in that way. But I know that for the family and for Daniel these contacts have been vital. He has always been part of their family and will remain so. On the second visit, being conscious of his family for the first time, he spent the first week hugging everyone in sight, assuming that he had found yet another cousin, aunt or uncle.

Indeed for Cameroonians Daniel is a Cameroonian, and on our second visit people would ask, 'When are you coming home to live?' This of course is false. Daniel is first and foremost British, and Britain is where he lives. It has been important that his other home is there for him in the future if he wants to be part of it, but for most of his life Daniel lives with a white mother. I believe that I have made choices in life which make this less problematic than it might have otherwise been. I have spent most of my working life concerned with issues related to race and racism, and as a result relevant subjects come up for discussion with relative ease. Secondly, we live in a multi-racial area of London, where being black is part of the norm. I am eternally grateful to our much maligned local authority for creating institutional support for schools such as Daniel's junior school which were prepared both to discuss and to outlaw racist behaviour as they did other forms of abuse and bullying. Daniel's friends had family ties with all parts of continental Europe, the Indian sub-continent, the Caribbean and Africa, and holidays in Pakistan or Cyprus, or Ghana were as common as trips to Clacton. Daniel has an entirely cosmopolitan view of the world. At the same time, through talking about other people's experiences, discussing racism as it is presented in the media or elsewhere, he has a realistic grasp of the nature of racism in our society, without having to experience it at a deep personal level in ways which would undermine his self-esteem or self-confidence.

He has been fortunate in having little direct experience of racism, but this has not occurred without effort. His school was chosen with care. I ran a mile from one where the headteacher referred me to the remedial teacher when I asked about multi-cultural education. And I have grave misgivings about ever moving from London. One of the few incidents which have distressed Daniel in relation to his being black happened in an Oxford playscheme, where some children called him names. Rushing to the playleader, expecting the support he would have found in his London school playground, he found that they brushed the incident aside. He was full of moral indignation. 'If it happens again,' he told me, 'I shall wait for their parents, and tell them, and ask them how they would like it.'

His reaction convinces me that I am not simply unaware of other incidents. There have in fact been very few. Our part of London, and I mean the very local area, does not have noticeable levels of street racism. The atmosphere is a friendly one, and tension-free. Unfortunately, this has meant that I have gained little experience in dealing with these situations in an appropriate manner. I have little hesitancy in reacting to racial abuse when it is directed at others, but when confronted with racism directed against Daniel and myself, my breath has been taken away so entirely that I have dissolved into speechlessness. One of the earliest incidents was when Daniel was in a pushchair, hardly more than a baby. Waiting for a tube train, a young couple with two small children walked past us, obviously disapproving, along the empty platform. The little girl, about four years old, detached herself, ran back and sang 'Nig, nog, sitting on a log!' Then 'Ugh! He's got brown feet.' I was speechless, looking at my beautiful baby, my mind reeling with feelings of distaste and sadness for the child.

I do feel inadequate, and it is easy to forget the need to mantain levels of discussion and support. I am white, I have no personal training in reacting to racist abuse, and if Daniel had his black family here, I am sure this would give him a better grounding. To a certain extent he is having to work out his own rules for responding to such situations, and I can only support him. As well as his own friends, he has my own friends to provide role models for being black in this society, but only too often it is true that he is surrounded by white people, and he comments on it. (Reading this, Daniel says, 'You are different Mum, because you can actually understand what it is like to be black in this country which most people don't.' I don't know that I can fully understand, but I am glad it feels like that.)

For me one of the most important things has been to give Daniel an enormous amount of self-esteem and confidence in himself, and I think I have done that. Perhaps too well, some might say, but I believe that he will need it on the day that racism properly knocks on his door.

Indeed, we have already encountered a full range of reactions to us as a family unit, given that Daniel is black and I am white. At one end of the spectrum there is overt revulsion. As one stranger who approached me in the park said, 'I can see that you love your baby, but how could you have done such a thing?' I have no answers for such people, not even anger, because we feel so totally right together it never occurs to me to refer to others for their views. At a personal level, their hang-ups are simply not my concern. Less extreme, there is no doubt that people make assumptions about us simply because of our skin colour. One of these assumptions has been that Daniel is adopted. One person asked me, 'When did you get him?' which rather dumbfounded me. A friend told me that she had only recently realised how alike we looked, and had assumed because Daniel was black, that he looked like his father. Then there are assumptions made that because I am a single parent, the relationship between Daniel's father and me did not work, or could not work, which is in no way the whole truth. Pierre-Marie has visited London three times now, and this year Daniel is planning to visit Cameroon on his own for the first time. It has worked exactly as we planned. Pierre-Marie and I are still loving friends, and do meet crazily and romantically at airports every few years! So perhaps for these reasons I feel a particular happiness when we are all together – as if that is a more complete statement.

Summing up

People make assumptions and retain stereotypes about single parenting as if it were a single identifiable thing. Whereas, even for Daniel and myself, it has contained many different facets, and taken us into different life styles: the early child-centred days, struggling financially, but when my career still seemed to be on course; a later stage when I had a well-paid job, Daniel started school and we expanded our family; then the next period when I left work to spend more time with Daniel developing his interests and found myself directed unexpectedly into new avenues of research and writing and finding a new creativity for myself.

Now we have entered a new phase. Having won a scholarship to a music school, Daniel is away at school during the week, a slow path towards separation and independence for both of us as the possibilities emerge to plan our futures independently of each other. In all this the stereotype of single parent families, responsible for society's ills, so heavily drawn on in government and official documents, is a foreign notion to me, and seems to bear no relation to our own condition or experience. I have a loving, outgoing, funny, talented child, whose life is full of friends and activity and whose experience of growing up outside a so-called traditional nuclear family has been enriching.

Daniel and I have together read through what I have written here. He says it is the way it is, and we cried together over it. I'm not sure I understand why, despite all the happiness, it feels so painful at times. I know there have been mistakes which I would not want to repeat. There have been contradictions, there may be unresolved feelings about it for both of us, but however I look at it, the path I chose seems the right one, almost inevitable.

GETTING MYSELF BACK

VIVETTE FERGUSON

I was 24 when I had my son, Daniel. I had known Bernie for quite a long time and, although I was still living with my mother, we had plans for getting married, buying a house and so on. It wasn't entirely an accident when I became pregnant. I knew that I wanted children and, as my mother had been 43 when she had me, I had clear ideas about having children while I was still fairly young.

Bernie hadn't gone on to further education whereas I had trained to be a teacher and I think this difference was very important in terms of our relationship. He is an electronic engineer, working at mending televisions, hi-fis and so on. He did do a couple of evening classes but never finished the courses and I think he found it highly stressful that I was a teacher and he had left school at 15. But at the time I was in love, and I didn't realise the implications of all this.

I went off to Jamaica for a holiday after my first year of teaching and it was when I returned that I became pregnant. I was bombarded by letters from Bernie during the six weeks that I was away which made me feel that our relationship had a definite future. My son was kind of planned and not planned and I felt OK about becoming pregnant because I hadn't yet got stuck into teaching. So together we set up home. However, I was playing at being a housewife and I hated it because I dislike housework so much. My enjoyment of being with Daniel was based on knowing that there was an end to it, that I was going to go back to work. I have always wanted to be a teacher, and have never wanted to be anything else, ever. I used to play schools when I was a child. I am fulfilling a desire that has always been there and even now, when things are so much worse in teaching, I have never felt that I wanted to get out.

However, as an unmarried, black teacher I have had to be very strong to persevere in teaching. Being unmarried has been one of the biggest things affecting the way other people react to me. In spite of this, I have never ever called myself Mrs anything – I'm always Miss. The bonus of being an unmarried mother was that it meant I had something in common with many of the mothers of the children I taught.

When Daniel was 1 year old and I was ready to go back to work, I did not want to go back to the school at which I had previously been teaching. The head-teacher there was a man who believed that if you had not been to university (I had qualified at a college of education), then you could not be a very good teacher. During the very early stages of my pregnancy, he was giving out posts of responsibility and, in my stupidity and honesty, I had told him that I was pregnant. I was just cut dead after that. I felt I could wave bye-bye to any possibilities of promotion. I also felt it was significant that, although there were many black children in the school, I was the only black teacher.

ILEA allocated me to another school and I found a parent there who also worked as a childminder. This was ideal and she looked after Daniel for over two years before he went into the nursery class. The head-teacher of the school was very sympathetic and understanding about my situation, even though she had no children of her own. When I first went to work at that school, there was only one other teacher who had any children, and she was working part-time. Most of the others were married but they were more concerned with their careers than with having families. It was a peculiar situation to be in, although as time went by it changed and more of the staff had children.

However, as the only teacher in the school at that time with a baby I found it a real struggle. I couldn't stay on for meetings very easily, or go to the pub after meetings. I notice now that, after staff meetings, it's the thinking and talking that goes on after the meeting that's really important.

The responsibility for looking after my child was entirely mine. I couldn't even rely on Bernie to collect Daniel from the childminder. If I collected Daniel myself and took him home, having asked Bernie to be there to look after him so that I could go out again, I found that I would be waiting for him to come back. After a while I gave up trying to rely on him.

Bernie didn't smoke or drink very much but he just liked the company of other men. He would sit around in a pub or someone else's house for hours just chatting. After we had been living together for two or three years, when the home was more comfortable, he started bringing his friends back to our place. They would come along, sometimes just because they had got something they wanted him to repair, and they would sit and chat for hours. I would come in tired from work, with Daniel. I was expected to chat to them, and to provide them with food and drink. In some ways I was very placid, but in other ways I made clear that there were things that I would not do. I soon got a reputation for not being as co-operative as some other women, in that mine was the one house where these men knew they would not have someone offering them food and drink, making them feel comfortable.

Bernie would very rarely come shopping with me so I got very adept at pushing a trolley and a buggy at the same time. I hated doing supermarket shopping so I would do one large shop which would last for a while. However, because I had no car, I had to get a taxi home and I always found this a problem. I would stand outside the supermarket and the taxi drivers would ignore me. There would be other women – white women – standing there, with twice as many bags as me, and they would have no trouble getting a taxi. Sometimes, a white friend would hail a taxi for me and then, telling the driver she was just going to get her bags, she would come and get me. It may be funny to talk about it now but at the time it was very hurtful.

Bernie was not interested in caring for Daniel. He liked showing him off, once he was clean and dressed. He would walk down the road exhibiting his wonderful son but he was never the sort of father who would take him off to a museum or the park for the afternoon. He still saw himself as a single person, a man about town. He went out a lot, partying and so on. Initially this was a social life we had together but, after two or three years, he would go on his own, leaving me at home with Daniel.

During the first few years of Daniel's life, I knew that I wanted another child but I sensed the relationship with Bernie would not last. It was a dilemma because I felt I would not want to commit myself to another man or to create a situation where my children had different fathers, so I felt that it was only within this relationship with Bernie that I could have another child. When Naomi was conceived, therefore, she was not actually planned but I wanted her very much.

The relationship had been strained for some time and finally a friend told me that he was seeing another woman. She would telephone the flat a lot and it got to the point where he was out more than he was in. Although I had been very tolerant, I eventually decided I would not carry on washing his clothes for him just so that he could go off with her, pretending he was a single man. Once I stopped doing his laundry he spent more time at his mother's house because she did it for him.

I had never felt part of his mother's family. His mother was a Christian and I am also a Christian but I never felt welcomed by her. Although she had not blamed me for being unmarried, she had never really confided in me or treated me as a daughter. Then, one Sunday when I visited her she told me she had found a lump in her breast. I persuaded her to go to the doctor, who immediately sent her to hospital. They operated on her but she never recovered. Bernie called me at school to tell me she had died but that I was not to come to the hospital. Of course, I immediately went down there and I found him there with another woman, Sandra. This was the woman with whom he had been having a relationship for some time.

I used to fantasise about meeting her. I had known that she existed and I wondered what it would be like if I ever met her. And now I was confronted with the situation. I thought it was important that I didn't lose my cool and have a slanging match with her or with him. When we left the hospital, he took Sandra back to his mother's house where all the relatives were gathered. There were no other women members of the family to organise things so I did all that – looking after the church members and so on. I was behaving calmly and thinking to myself, why should I wait for him to decide which of us he wants? I can decide.

When I walked through the door of Bernie's mother's house on the day of the funeral and saw that Sandra was there, I knew that Bernie no longer felt that Daniel and I were important to him. He was demonstrating this by his action of inviting her to such a significant family occasion. At that moment I also knew that I didn't have the love that I used to have for him any more. The betrayal was so great. I realised that he must have taken Sandra to his mother's house many times, and his mother must have known about their relationship. I had thought that I had a place within that family and yet all the time that place was being usurped. I felt betrayed by Bernie and by his family.

The thing that really finished it for me was something which was seemingly trivial but which symbolised Bernie's unacceptable behaviour. Sandra was going to go to the funeral in a see-through dress. That was what did it. I thought he should have more sense than to be with someone who behaved so inappropriately. I told her she could not go dressed like that and that she had to put a petticoat on. I felt that if Bernie could not see that her behaviour was wrong, then he was not worth all this hassle.

The scene at the hospital after Bernie's mother had died and at the house on the day of the funeral, have remained in my mind, like snapshots. They were both turning points in my feelings for Bernie, and had a lasting impact on my life since then.

However, by the day of the funeral I knew that I was pregnant, and afterwards we sat down and talked about it. He questioned whether the child was his. He never lived with us after that although he spent a lot of time at the flat and continued to be there off and on for two years after my daughter was born. During those two years our relationship cooled right down. It felt so strange to me that physically he looked the same but I no longer had the same feelings for him. Sex had always been a very good part of our relationship but now my desire for him waned. I realised that he was behaving as a 'young stud about town', and that whereas I had matured as I grew older he had not.

I don't think Bernie ever properly accepted that Naomi was his. I've heard that he told other people that I was trying to trap him into staying with me and that I must think he was a fool to be deceived into thinking that she was his child. He is a kind and gentle person but he is also an abuser of people's caring and his own lack of caring helped to make the first three years of Naomi's life very difficult.

He was there the day that I came out of hospital after Naomi was born, because he had been looking after Daniel, but he then went off for the evening. I was fine because all my women friends came round that evening, but he wasn't to know that and I've never forgotten that he left me there on my own. Life was very difficult at that time and, looking back on it now, I don't know how I managed.

I went back to work when Naomi was 9 weeks old, for financial reasons. However, I couldn't find a childminder. A neighbour looked after her for a while but she suddenly gave up doing it at half-term and I had only a week to find someone else. I got very depressed; so much so that I wondered what was the point of living. Another neighbour who was very supportive had a nanny and I sent Naomi to her for a while, but it cost £40 a week (this was in 1980). Bernie wasn't contributing anything towards the children, or the rent, or the bills. I put Naomi's name down for the council nursery but they told me I did not qualify because, although I was a single parent, I was in work. So, in desperation, I took her along one morning and left her there. I said that if they didn't like it they could call the police. She was given a place after that. I was so relieved because otherwise I would have had to resign my job.

I was ill for a lot of Naomi's first year. I had mastitis when she was only a month old and had to stop breastfeeding. Then I was in a lot of pain which was finally diagnosed as gall stones but I couldn't have the operation because it would mean leaving Naomi and not being able to look after her for some weeks afterwards. Finally, when Naomi was a year old I had to have my gall bladder out because the pain had got so bad. Bernie looked after her and Daniel then but he didn't bring the children to see me very often; it felt like he was too busy. I was very aware that he was failing to look after Naomi properly. He fed the children hamburgers and chips all the time, which was not such a problem for Daniel because he was five but Naomi was too young for that kind of food. I felt dreadful. The experience completely ruined Naomi's sleeping and eating patterns. The worst thing was that she did not have a first birthday party as I was admitted to hospital the day before she was a year old. I had no time to prepare anything because I was told only the day before I went in that they had a bed for me.

During that time, I felt I was betraying my daughter. I had spent a whole year with Daniel after he was born but I had returned to work when Naomi was only nine weeks old. And then on her first birthday I was not even there. I felt Naomi had not been given the kind of bonding with me that Daniel had. I also feel that Bernie never accepted her as his own child and that his neglect of her was partly because of this. I don't think he harmed her but he just did not care enough.

Naomi was 2 years old when Bernie and I finally split up. I had got to the stage where, one weekend when he went to see Sandra's parents in Kent, I even packed his bag for him. It felt very therapeutic; every time I put something in the bag it was a little bit of our life that I was putting in there. One morning soon after that, I told him that he had to decide. He should either give me the keys to the flat now and go or he should decide that he was here as a part of this family. I thought if he had no keys he wouldn't have free access to the flat. He didn't want to give the keys up because he wanted us there and his other life as well, but I insisted that he chose between the two. We had been through a phase when he had not been at the flat for a few weeks and I had got into a routine without him. The children were more settled. I had got a teaching post of responsibility and I was just beginning to see the light at the end of tunnel. Then he had come back and our lives were disrupted again. My feelings got all churned up and I thought I can't cope with this, it's too up and down. It also unsettled the children. I did not think he had anything to offer them apart from his physical presence – which he only offered in short bursts, anyway.

So he left. I told him that he could see the children every other weekend and that on those weekends he could even stay at the flat. He agreed to this but after coming three times he missed two visits. It was coming up for Christmas and he promised the children presents which never materialised. Moreover, he promised to bring the Christmas tree but didn't bring it until 1 am on Christmas Day, and then he expected to stay. That was it. I told him that if he could not come regularly then he could not come at all and that it was his decision.

He then stopped coming to see the children. However, on Naomi's third birthday, he brought some flowers for her. By that time, my friend Sue, whom I worked with, had moved into the flat. She had started to stay there during the train strike but then moved in to live with us during termtime. It worked very well because it meant I was not in the situation of talking to children all day and then having no adult to talk to during the evening. What is more, she liked cooking.

At Naomi's party, Bernie started saying in a loud voice that he didn't like the company. He had been told by friends that Sue had moved in and he assumed that there was a sexual relationship going on between us. One night soon after that, he came round, drunk and banging on the door. I let him in and and he had his hands all over me. He came up the stairs saying that he shouldn't have done what he did, he really did love me, his hands all over my body. I felt so violated that it was almost like being raped. Sue and the kids were upstairs so I let him into the living room and tried to deal with the situation without involving them. Looking back on it I think he had come to find out where Sue and I were sleeping, whether we were sharing a bed.

He did not understand that women can have much closer relationships with each other than men have with other men without it necessarily being a sexual relationship. Once I had let him into the living room he wanted to have sex with me. I don't think he knew how strong I was. I kneed him in the groin and chucked him out – which I feel very good about. As he was going he called me a lesbian. He telephoned me a couple of times after that and shouted the word down the telephone and then he came round one day to pick up a television that was still in the flat and screamed that I was a lesbian. I was really worried that he would make trouble for me at work. It is bad enough being a black unmarried mother as a teacher, but if I was thought to be a lesbian I was afraid things could get very unpleasant.

I have not seen him at all for eight years now, and neither have the children. About four years ago, he passed a message to me via a mutual friend, saying, 'I am doing all right now and I would like to see the children.' When I received the message I was so angry. I thought the cheek of it, I'm bringing these kids up and he's made no contribution at all. And he thinks that he can suddenly walk back into our lives. I didn't want to know him anymore.

After Bernie left for good, I gave my children a lot of sheltering and a lot of support. I did not have much social life myself but we went out a lot together. I have often wondered what life would have been like if he had not left. I do not think he would have changed; he would still have been going around with other women and this would have been worse for the children. I think that in a sense I have had the best of both worlds because I have been able to have children and yet have been able to organise my own life and to give the children stability.

Naomi never really knew her father but Daniel did. He very quickly realised that his father let him down because he didn't turn up for visits or to bring Christmas or birthday presents when he said he would. My son is a very sensitive and caring lad. He never once said, 'Where is Daddy?' Why hasn't he come back?' I have never talked to him properly about his father. I haven't said nasty things about Bernie but neither have we spoken about him generally – although I do often say things like 'You've got hands like your father's'. There are things about Daniel that remind me of his father – he likes boxing and snooker and I say to him, 'Your father likes that.'

Now my son is coming up to 15 years old I think he may want to get in touch with his father. I feel all right about that because I have given Daniel a secure family life and it is up to him to decide whether he would like to have the kind of life style that his dad has. However, if Daniel were actually to say that he wants to see his father, then I think we would need to talk and to get things clear. I don't think the children know that Bernie left us to be with someone else. Instead, I have given them the impression that he wasn't ready to be a father, that the responsibility of having a regular income and looking after children was too much for him at that stage in his life. And this is true, really.

I felt it was important not to make him out to be a rotten, horrible man because at some point I did love him and he is the father of my children. I still want him to be a good person in my children's eyes. However, I don't think it is a big issue for them that their father is not part of their lives. I think that it is just that he is not there and that's it.

I love children but I can't have any more as I had a hysterectomy four years ago. I would have loved to have more children but I knew I never would as it would mean having two children with one person and then one or two with another. It's in my nature that if I love someone I love them deeply and passionately, and I don't think I have ever stopped physically loving Bernie. That's probably partly why I have never committed myself to any other man.

I have been celibate now for seven years. When Bernie left I wanted time on my own. I had feelings of failure as a mother, as a lover, as a person. I had made him leave but essentially he had rejected me. I needed time to get back my own self-esteem. I think you give up part of yourself when you enter into a relationship and I needed to get myself back. Having got myself back I'm not sure I ever want to give it to anyone else. It would be nice to have relationship but I don't ever want to give my whole body and soul to anyone else again. The experience of being rejected meant that I spent some time getting back my confidence and self-esteem and now I feel a whole person on my own.

I am now 38 years old and a deputy headteacher. I have had great satisfaction throughout my seventeen years of teaching in Hackney, Camden and Islington. I am beginning to apply for headships and am fairly confident that I will eventually get one.

My career has given me an independence I would not otherwise have been able to achieve. Combining family and work has been difficult but I wouldn't have had it any other way. My son will be sitting his GCSEs next year and my daughter starts secondary school this September. With my car – I passed my test on the fourth attempt and didn't drive for nine years afterwards – I now have even greater freedom. I am looking forward to driving to Scotland in the summer and Spain in the autumn.

BECOMING A SINGLE PERSON

SINDHU HOPE

I am 40 years old and I have four children, aged 18, 15, 12 and 7. I had my first child on my own having become pregnant six weeks after meeting his father. He was in the middle of the break-up of his first marriage and we separated when I was four months pregnant. He had not resolved the situation with his first wife and they wanted to try and repair/maintain their marriage, as they had a 2 year old child.

They did not manage to do so and, two years later, he finally decided that he wanted a relationship with me. We lived together for the next thirteen years, having another three children together, before we separated in 1988. I spent most of my marriage at home, as a traditional middle-class wife and mother. In 1986 I began a degree course, finishing in 1990 and I am now training to be a teacher.

As I write, I find it difficult to define for myself what a single parent is. I cannot separate my parenting from who I am, a single person who also has children. My experience as a single parent is inextricably bound up with who I am, who I have become.

In a sense I wanted to be a parent before I wanted to be my own person. When I was 23, I was extremely passive and child-like, unsure of myself, and afraid of being alive in the world. Yet I was sure of wanting a child. I felt strong and confident of my ability to mother. Becoming a mother was the only way I could visualise myself. I was determined to be able to mother in the way I felt right. This was a paradox as in most other areas I was so unsure and unable.

In retrospect I find it sad that I couldn't visualise myself any other way, that I had no perception of motherhood being one choice among many. I feel this was partly owing to the time in which I grew up and partly owing to my personal emotional history. I needed to have a child in order to define myself as an adult.

Over the years I was forced to confront and come to terms with who I was, apart from – or as well as – being a wife and mother. After years of turmoil and indecision I realised and accepted that I could not remain in my marriage *and* be true to myself. The sense of who I was as a person and what I needed or wanted from my life became a more pressing reality than that of being a wife and mother. I had become aware that I was attempting to maintain a situation that nurtured others but not myself. It was the difference between always seeing myself in relation to others, putting others first, and, in contrast, acknowledging the value of my sense of self which had its own imperatives. These imperatives could not be reconciled within my marriage, so I came to recognise that I had no other choice but to end the marriage.

My first thought when faced with writing about single parenthood was that I am not a real single parent. I realised that I carry an unconscious image of what constitutes a single parent: poverty, youth, bad housing, no support network, shabby, sad, stressed and depressed. I surprise myself!

My ex-husband sees the children and makes a contribution to their maintenance but, with regard to the everyday on-going practical and emotional work of parenting, I am a single parent. When I consider the implications and reality of that, I realise that to a large degree I was so even when I lived with my children's father. Perhaps there is a sense in which the majority of traditional wives/mothers are in reality single parents?

In my marriage, there was a very clear demarcation of roles. My husband earned the money, dealt with 'the world', and attended to all household maintenance. I had responsibility for everything else – primarily childcare. Childcare and the constraints of parenting were an optional extra for him. My life was fragmented by attending to others, his could follow an uninterrupted flow.

When I had my first child in 1973 we were not single parents, but unmarried mothers. At the ante-natal clinic they insisted on calling me Mrs, even after I had asked them not to. At each visit the sister would take me into a room and talk at me about having the baby adopted. She would say. 'It's not fair to bring up a child without a father – don't you think you're being very selfish? You won't be able to give the baby a proper home or family life.'

These remarks did not have much affect on me in terms of my confidence to mother my child. However, they did add to the pain and insecurity of my situation. And they did reinforce my perception of myself as a deficient person.

I was homeless until I was eight months pregnant – staying with friends – then I got a room in a short life house. A few months after the birth I moved to a friend's house, renting a room. Later still I got a flat in another short life house. I lived on social security with a token contribution from the baby's father, but during this time I hardly saw him.

I loved becoming a mother and on the whole enjoyed having the baby on my own. I enjoyed the freedom to immerse myself in providing and caring for him without the conflicting pull of anyone else's needs or demands. I loved the feeling of being a self-contained unit – just the two of us. I didn't at that time ask much more of my life.

What terrified me, though, was the reality of his dependence on me – the reality of his aloneness without me. Night after night I would dream or fantasise a scenario where I was dead, he was alone and no one knew. He would lie in his cot crying and no one would come. However, the positive sides of mothering far outweighed the negative. I was utterly enraptured with my baby. And the wonder of creation and nurture. That from my body, my milk, he grew.

Having my second child – in a relationship with love, support, good housing – was emotionally far harder. I had to cope with the difficulty of fulfilling the expectations and demands of being a wife, lover and mother. For me those were in many ways conflicting roles. They were conflicting for many reasons – I was 'in love' with my baby and yet I could not immerse myself in her in the way that I had with my first child, because my husband needed/wanted me. I recognise it was partly my immaturity that made it difficult to fulfil both roles, but I think it was also the underlying current of his jealousy and need. He saw me primarily as his wife/lover. I saw myself primarily as my children's mother.

Being a wife meant providing a clean and ordered home, meals cooked, clothes washed, children ready for bed. My husband had to have undisturbed sleep because he had to work. There were also the tensions over different conceptions of shared parental responsibilities. These became greater over the years, particularly when my husband's daughter came to live with us when she was 12. In many ways we had fundamentally different views of what was appropriate parenting and I felt he was not prepared to accept what I thought were many of the responsibilities and constraints involved in bringing up children.

I chose to leave the relationship – because of other issues as well as those of parenting – so in that sense I was not a reluctant single parent. The decision was motivated by my needs as a person not as a parent.

Initially I wallowed in a new-found freedom. Freedom from the tension and distress of an unhappy situation. Freedom to decide how and when I would do what I wanted; to deal with the children in the way I felt best without it causing arguments and conflict; to have the children sleep in my bed if they wanted to.

Then I began to settle into the everyday slog. The anxiety about money that kept me awake for hours at night. The overwhelming number of things to be done, continually, with no respite. Even though I had felt myself emotionally a single parent within my marriage, my husband had made important practical and material contributions. Now I had to deal not only with running a household and caring for children, but also with providing the majority of the finances. I had to fix anything that broke (and everything seemed to break suddenly), deal with mortgages and insurance companies and so on, and study for second-year exams.

I was outnumbered by the children and felt overhelmed by the dynamics of their relationships with each other, as well as by the expression of their neediness, loss and anger. My eldest son, then 15, became very aggressive and confrontational. I cried a lot, doubted my decision and felt I would never be able to cope. I wrote a poem in my journal at that time.

Feel as though
I'm standing in a desert
after a sandstorm
has
obliterated the road.

I also recorded a dream that I had. 'I dreamt I was walking beside a river. The river swollen, the water covering the bank. I had to get into the water. It was very deep. Rushing. There were rocks hidden. I was afraid but I had to get in.' This dream epitomises that period of time – my fear of being overwhelmed and yet having to plunge in. I had always in my life up to then felt ineffectual, frail, lacking. Years of being at home had eroded my confidence. Within my marriage, my perception of my reality had been consistently undermined so that I found it difficult to trust myself, to have faith in myself. I felt like a shadow.

Through doing a degree course, my confidence increased. I spent a lot of time thinking back and reviewing my life. I began to see past events and situations with quite a new perspective. I started to validate perceptions and feelings which I had denied or relinquished. Through taking control of my decisions and choices, and taking responsibility for my material existence, I began to acquire a strong sense of my self and my capabilities. I started to realise that I could cope, that I could more than just cope – I could make a life for us.

Being there for your children through a period when they are experiencing loss and anger is very hard. Particularly when you are seen as the one who has destroyed their family. They need you to be strong, sure and encompassing when you too feel loss, anger and vulnerability, when you feel unsure whether you have made the right decision. Children have no choice; their lives are changed by adult decisions. It is only very gradually that they become aware that they have survived and that what was initially felt as devastation can in fact prove to be positive change. Only gradually did I come to trust that my decision was the right one for me – and therefore for them, because they share my everyday reality.

My becoming a lone mother has changed our lives enormously. The shape of our family is changing. Indeed what it means to be a family is still emerging. One of my daughters has said, 'We're not a family any more.' I found that painful and somehow diminishing of me and my efforts. She, however, is expressing an opinion that is shaped by loss, and the outside world; shaped by the perception and expectation that a family without two parents (male and female) is not real, is lacking, is not enough.

My children are the most important concern of my life right now. They are not my life in that I have other interests, ties, commitments, but they are central. And I do well enough by them. I am proud of my mothering and it has been one of the most enriching and rewarding aspects of my life. The children are a source of great joy and, since being on my own with them, I have become more aware of that and appreciative of them.

We are all volatile, strong willed and strongly opinionated people, which makes for conflict. Life is not quiet in our house. The raw emotion (particularly with two teenage daughters) is an aspect which I find hardest. It is a struggle not to feel diminished or submerged, and to maintain a strong and positive sense of myself and my way. It is in relation to these issues that I feel most acutely my single status. There is no one to discuss these things with, no one to be there for them when they hate you – no one else to be the monster for a while. There is no one supporting me in dealing with it. This is the isolation of being on your own. I feel that it's not that I particularly need a partner so much as access to, and interaction with, other adults. It's difficult to get out often and I'm exhausted. I begin to get caught in a spiral of feeling down and wanting company, at the same time as not wanting company because I'm feeling down. Being the sole adult is a lot of effort – consistent, insistent effort.

I would have preferred, throughout my life as a mother, to have shared parenting in an equal and committed way. Or I would like to think that is what I wanted. It is not a clear issue for me. On the one hand, I had no model for shared parenting in my family in that my father was there physically but my mother did all the parenting. When I was younger I wanted/needed my children to be 'mine'. On the other hand my ex-husband and I had such different understandings of what is 'good' parenting. He seems to have forgotten what it feels like to be a child, and seems unable to give full weight or credence to what children feel, say and do. In many ways, he expects his children to give him consideration, reassurance, support and understanding, or he wants to be 'friends' with them. Our different understandings of what constitutes appropriate parenting remains an unresolved isssue.

Being a single parent is not a state – it is a process. It changes as you and your children grow. People are single parents through a variety of circumstances and situations, at particular points in their lives. And we are many-faceted people as well as parents. I experience being a lone parent in relation to the situation from which I came, and in relation to the children's continuing relationship with their father, and therefore my relationship with him around them. I am affected by many dynamics beyond that of being solely a single parent.

WRITING TO STOP THE HURT

MARY JOHN

When I get depressed and the past keeps coming back to hurt me, I find it easier to write about what happened to me than to talk about it. Often it is easier to write about things as if they have happened to someone else and not to me. Writing does not make me forget about things but it stops them hurting so much. Afterwards I feel much better.

I came to this country from St Lucia when I was 14 years old.

> She used to live in a dream world where her mother was a beautiful woman who loved her, and her sisters, brother and stepdad were just waiting for her to be one happy family. She couldn't wait to be with them. She used to dream that she would make lots of friends in a new school.
>
> It was on a cold, frosty morning in December when she met her stepdad, mother and sister at the airport. Her stepdad was the only one who spoke to her. He told her that he was her stepdad and this lady was her mother. When she saw her she wished she could run and go back to her lovely beautiful grandmother. Her dream was soon to turn into a nightmare.
>
> All the housework was left for her to do while the rest of the family lived like kings and queens. When she went to school for the first time it was no better. The children laughed at her and called her names because of the clothes she had to wear. She did not have anyone to turn to. So going to school was another nightmare.
>
> The first summer in London her stepdad got her a job in a factory. The hours were from eight to five. She hated the job. All her wages went to her mum. Between family, school and

the job, they had turned a once happy, outspoken child into a withdrawn depressed child.

One day her mother told her she had a heart like a devil.

Now she has got a family of her own. But nothing has changed. Her family is still the same. Only her two older sisters keep in touch with her. She finds herself lonely and hasn't got any confidence in herself, because, at 14, all of it was gone. She feels anger and hurt at the way they treated her.

She will never forgive them.

I am 29 years old and I have two boys and a girl. I have been a single mum for nine years. I first left my sons' father when I was three months pregnant because he used to drink and used to beat me up. When I got my flat, a friend told him where I was so he used to hang around the flats. I used to be so scared that I let him move in. By that time my older son was about 3 months old. I then became pregnant with my other son. The drinking did not stop or the beatings.

She sat in the kitchen smoking a cigarette, nervously watching the clock. He would soon be home. The children had been in bed for over an hour.

She was wondering for how long she could take the beating and shouting. He had been so like a dream when they first met but once they got married it all changed. He usually came home drunk and took it out on her or shouted at the children. She started putting the children to bed early, but once the shouting started they would soon be awake.

She jumped from a thought as she heard the front door slam. He came in the kitchen. 'Where's my dinner?' he asked as she got up to get it from the oven. 'Where're the children?' She told him they were in bed. 'Why are they always in bed when I come home?' 'Because they had a long day at school.' She put the dinner down in front of him, then turned to put the kettle on. The next thing she knew she was being dragged by the hair. He kicked, punched her in the face and stomach. She was on the floor. He started throwing anything he could find at her. Upstairs the children were awake. They knew better than to go downstairs. They pulled the covers over their heads and hoped that he would soon stop. Downstairs he grabbed a beer from the fridge and sat down to watch the TV.

She started to clean up the kitchen and hoped he would fall

asleep. Then she went into the bathroom. What she saw was not new to her: two black eyes, a burst lip and a bump on her head. She found it difficult to walk. She did not know how she made it to bed. She knew that she had to get away or he would kill her.

The next day he dropped the children at school on the way to work because he didn't want anyone to see his wife with black eyes. While he was out she packed a few things and the children's clothes and then phoned the London Federation for Battered Women. They gave her a number to call which was out of her area. She rang them and they told her to come straight away. She phoned the school and asked them if she could pick the children up early.

One hour later she was on the train to a new life and prayed that he would not try and find her. She was very nervous and frightened in case someone saw her and told him where she was going.

When she arrived at the refuge she discovered that some women had been through worse than her.

When my second son was born I went into a refuge for battered women. Then I met my daughter's dad and I went out with him for seven years. But my ex-boyfriend found out where I was living and set my letter box on fire. I then went back into the refuge. After a year there I was rehoused.

Anyone who hasn't been in a refuge does not know the courage it takes to walk out of your home, family and friends to go and live in a house that you have to share with other women and their children. Children running up and down, jumping up and down on the settee, walking over the units in the kitchen when you're trying to watch TV. The worst thing is when a child comes in and switches the TV over. The best thing to do is to get a TV and put it in your room. But it is very hard to keep children in their room all day. Sometimes you ask yourself what you would do if there was a fire.

There were some women who would leave their children in their room and go out all night. Sometimes they would bring men back to the house which was stupid, foolish and disrespectful to the other women and children in the house. Some women and children are terrified of men because of what they have been through.

There used to be a house meeting every week to work out your differences but it wouldn't take long before one woman started to cause trouble all over again: like telling the new woman about someone else in the house. Then that new woman would go and tell the other woman that she had heard that someone said something about her and, before you knew it, there was a war. It was like a bomb waiting to explode.

Sometimes you wanted to give up and go back to the beating because of the bitchiness. As well as all that you got pressure from the school, the DHSS and the housing authorities. Especially if you are a Catholic and your children are in a Catholic school. They make you feel guilty because you are in a refuge, and take it out on the children. The DHSS would make you go up and down to their office, make you wait for your money only to tell you that it is in the post and that you will get it the next day. The next day it still hasn't arrived and you would spend the weekend borrowing the money off the women in the house to feed your children. It would go on like that for weeks until they sent you the money.

The refuge workers are always there to talk to you. They give you the support and courage to go on and they try to do all they can to get you rehoused.

There was a playroom but the women wouldn't take the responsibility for looking after it. So, at the weekends, the workers locked it, which meant that the kids couldn't use it. The playworkers took the children out during the school holidays, letting the women have a break. After school they would take them swimming. Once they took the children and women to Cornwall for a week. While on holiday some of the small children used to walk in to a shop, take umbrellas and walk out with them. By the time we left we had about ten umbrellas that weren't paid for.

There was food going missing from the cupboard and fridge, money going missing out of the rooms – you had to keep your room locked at all times. Some women were not doing the work they were supposed to do. You would sometimes find one woman would be doing the job that two or three women were supposed to be doing.

There were good times and bad times. Sometimes we would buy wine or lager and sit down in the kitchen and have a party and tell each other stories about what we had been through. We used to have a laugh about it because we used to think that some men don't know what they're doing.

The house was big, and at night it was so quiet, especially at weekends. When you were in the house alone, it was so creepy that you wouldn't want to go downstairs. Then the phone would ring. When you ran down the stairs to pick it up, whoever was on the phone would not speak. They would put the phone down and they would keep on ringing until you picked it up and the same thing would happen again. The best thing to do was to take the phone off the hook, but that wasn't allowed because there could be a woman who needed a refuge and you couldn't send anyone away because there was an open-door policy.

When you got your own flat, it was worth having put up with all the difficulties.

It's only over the last year that I have really noticed that people think that because you are a single mum that you've got problems. The only problem I've got at the moment is that people offer me clothes and money. If they only knew how much it hurts, I'm sure they wouldn't offer it.

I am not working but I will never have to beg.

When I was in the refuge a social worker came to see me and told me that my son told them that I scratched him. I knew that I had done it. My children were put on the At Risk Register for one year. But this year, when they came and said I had hit my son, it was not true. They put the children on the At Risk Register again but this time I know I did not do it.

I am doing my best to bring my children up the right way. It is social workers who are causing me problems at the moment. I have been on my own a long time and I will keep on doing the best for my children until I die.

I have just done a one-year course in English and Word Processing and I hope to do another year and after that find a job. Then I want to take my children back to St Lucia.

I have been through a lot worse than what is happening now and I still came out on top. I will do it again. The most important thing to me is that my children are happy. I think people are waiting for me to say that I cannot cope but they will have a long wait because I've got a lot of courage to keep on going.

FEELING POSITIVE

ANGELA JULES

I was twenty-one when my daughter, Judith, was born, ten years ago. Her father, Godfrey, wasn't around at that time because he had gone over to the States to study accountancy. In fact he was already there when I discovered that I was pregnant. As he was a student, he couldn't help me financially. We kept in touch and there was an unspoken assumption that when he qualified we would be together. I suppose I would be lying if I didn't acknowledge that I did hope that we would have a future together.

However, I didn't think that being pregnant in itself was a reason for getting married. In the West Indies, where I come from, people don't get married just because a woman's pregnant. In many cases, a man and woman will get married after they've had children. In my situation, the appropriate time for us to get married would have been after he had qualified. Similarly, in the West Indies it is things other than children that determine when the right time is to get married. For most of the West Indian people that I know, marriage isn't a big thing in the way that it is for some white people. My mother says it's better to live together and be happy, than to be married and unhappy.

Luckily for me, I was still living at home with my mum and dad when I became pregnant. My mother knew before I did. I was three months pregnant before I went to the doctor to confirm what was going on. When I told my mother she said, 'Yes I know.' She didn't mind that I was pregnant as I was by then a qualified secretary (which had been her ambition for me) and, as she said, I could always go back to work afterwards. In fact, she suggested that she took her retirement when it was due, rather than take up the option of continuing with her job, so that I could get back to work. My father just accepted my pregnancy. My mother was the one who told him and he never mentioned it to me. The fact that he helped me financially with my daughter's christening made me think that he didn't mind about it.

There were times when I panicked, when I thought, 'Oh no. What am I going to do?' The thought of adoption went through my mind, but not abortion. I had to give up my job as a secretary because I had morning sickness for the entire nine months of my pregnancy. I also had to go into hospital six weeks before my daughter was born because I was losing weight. It was an awful pregnancy.

I didn't initially expect Godfrey to make any contribution to my daughter because he was a student. Luckily for me I had the support of my family. Even my sister in Canada said that if I didn't want to keep the child she would have her. We went over to the States to see Godfrey when Judith was 1½ years old. That was the first time he saw her. Everything was OK between us and then he came over when she was 4, which was also OK. However, when he went back, the letters from him weren't what I expected on the basis of what had gone on between us while he was over here. I read between the lines and thought that something was going on. I subsequently found out that he had got involved with another woman and he then moved in with her. A little while later they got married.

I had expected that when he qualified he would give some financial support for my daughter on a regular basis, but he didn't at first. Whenever any of my family went over to the States he would give them money for her but it was all very irregular and unpredictable. Then, three years ago, when he came over here for his brother's wedding, I tackled him and said that he ought to contribute to his daughter. He now pays a regularly monthly amount, although it is not very much and he has never increased it over the three years.

I am not really on speaking terms with him now because he hurt me too badly. I found out entirely by accident that he had moved in with this other woman. He wrote saying that he had moved but did not give me his telephone number. Eventually I got the number through another friend. When I telephoned, this woman answered. It was a horrible way to find out. I was very angry with him but now it's more that I just want him to acknowledge how much he hurt me. I still can't speak to him on an ordinary social level because he hasn't recognised what he did. People say that I'm still in love with him but I know I'm not. It's just that I want him to accept how much he hurt me, whereas as far as he is concerned he has done nothing wrong. I don't hold any malice against him; I have to get on with my life.

I stayed at home for about eighteen months after my daughter was born. I became a different person, physically and mentally, after her birth. I felt as if I had a responsibility that I had never had before. I didn't know whether to panic or what. But I enjoyed her and being at home with her, and wished that I never had to work again.

I went to the States with my family when my daughter was 18 months old, which was when I took her to see her father. My mother then took Judith to Canada for six months, to visit my sister – who was pregnant – while I came back to England and got a secretarial job in London. I missed my daughter but my mother was the best person to look after her. My mother is always looking after babies. When she came back to England she brought my sister's baby with her because my sister had two other young children and she was finding it difficult.

When I first moved down to London from Birmingham. I shared a flat with my other sister and, when my mother returned from Canada with Judith, I would go back home at weekends. This arrangement worked fine but after a while Judith started to want to come back to London with me. So, when she was due to go to school, I brought her down to London, by which time I had got a council flat. She went to a Catholic school near where I worked.

Two years ago, I decided I was fed up with being a secretary and I applied to do teacher training. I got someone who was a friend of a friend to come over from St Lucia to help me out with taking my daughter to school and picking her up because her school was a long way away from where the college was. She lived with us for a year, which was very helpful. It was very difficult financially as I paid her fare over here but I managed. My eldest sister would buy groceries for me and my brother would help out financially whenever he could.

Now I'm working part-time at a further education college and I've sent my daughter to a fee-paying school close by. It's a Seventh Day Adventist school and is run on the West Indian principles of education. This means that there are exams every term and that if the child doesn't pass the end of year exams she has to repeat the year. It's very strict and does all the things I hated in school in the West Indies, but now I realise how much better the educational standards are there. The school is mostly Black and has Black teachers. They teach Black history which is good, although that isn't the reason I sent my daughter there.

The school isn't just for Seventh Day Adventists, neither is it selective. Children take an entrance examination and their parents are interviewed. Whether they get accepted depends on whether the child has potential rather than how well they do in the exam and also, especially, on what the parents' attitude is. If you don't like your child being disciplined then you can forget it. They don't hit the children, apart from the odd smack, but they are very strict. For example, they have to wear the uniform and can't even wear a coloured ribbon in their hair, or trainers.

The teachers are very good at dealing with any problems that children may have, by talking to them. The classes are not that big, fewer than twenty, and they have two or three teachers per class. If children are held back from going up to the next class, they get the extra help they need so that they can achieve the standard to go up to the next class. I've learnt things from my daughter since she's been going there. She has homework every night which I have to help her with. She has to do grammar and she has a handwriting book. She's doing very well and I'm very pleased with the school.

My daughter never really took to her father at first, although she's OK with him now. I think the problem was that when he came over when she was 4 years old, he wanted to behave as a father immediately instead of getting to know her. He wanted to tell her off and things like that. She resented that. Now, he writes to her every month and she writes back, although I have to nag her to do this sometimes. I don't think she's particularly keen to go over to see him, except that she would like to go to Disneyland. She hasn't really missed out on having a father because she's got my father, whom she calls both Dad and Grandad. She also calls my mother Mum and Grandma.

She's very close to her father's brother. He spent a lot of time with her when she was younger. He recently had a child of his own and I said that he needn't feel he had to spend so much time with Judith, but he replied that she's his niece and of course he still wanted to spend time with her. He even wanted to pay some of her school fees but I wouldn't let him because he had just got married.

I've been living on my own for so long now it doesn't bother me. I had dated with men but nothing that developed into anything serious.

On the whole, I haven't come across racism, or any discrimination against me as a black unmarried mother and, as far as I know, my daughter has never encountered racism. Although her current school is mostly black, her previous school was mostly white and she didn't have any problems.

When I went on my teacher training course, I found out that there was research which showed that West Indian children underachieved at school. I was really shocked because this wasn't my perception at all. I found it very worrying. I felt I wanted to teach black children in order to give them a chance, and I also worried about my daughter. In the West Indies the parents can rely on the education system to bring out the best in children, whereas in this country I think schools assume that parents will sit down with children at home and encourage them to work hard. In the West Indies, that is left up the school. In this country, children need that extra push from parents and this is, I think, where West Indian children in Britain lose out because their parents aren't doing this – they assume that such encouragement is the school's business.

The majority of students I teach now are black and they are really lacking in motivation. They haven't received the encouragement from either the school or their parents and it's very sad. They are capable of learning but they just haven't got the motivation. Some West Indian parents are aware that they do need to push their children but many are not.

I want my daughter to go to university but I know I mustn't push her too hard. She tends to want to follow in my footsteps; when I was a secretary she wanted to be a secretary, now I'm a teacher she wants to be a teacher. I want her to do better than me, to go further than me.

I feel that single mothers should not feel downhearted or alone. We should enjoy our children. The stigma of being unmarried is just a label and I don't feel that all the negative things that are assumed to be part of being a single mother apply to me.

MARESA

CAROLINE MacKEITH

I chose to be a single parent. I was in my mid-30s, working at an interesting job as a practice nurse and health visitor. I had my own house and I wanted to be a mother. Over the next two years I had two pregnancies but miscarried both times. It was emotionally exhausting and I felt very low, but I still wanted to be a mother.

I thought of adoption as a single parent, but I was 39 by then and wondered if I would be allowed to. So I enquired about fostering. When the social worker came to see me, he was perceptive enough to pick up that I really wanted to adopt, and he explained that I would be allowed to adopt a 'special needs' child. 'Special needs' means any child over 5 years old and a child of any age who has a disability. I think that at the time in my area you would have had to be under 37 years old and a married couple to have been eligible for a child under 5 years old with no disability.

Initially I thought that I wanted either a child over 12 years of age or a child under 8. A 12 year old child is emerging from childhood and so we would start out with a different relationship, and under 8 years there are still some years of childhood left. I also said I would be happy to have a child with a disability. As time went on, I realised that I would rather have a young child. It is difficult to know exactly why I felt this. I think probably I wanted parenting to be a full-time job and I wanted to get to know a child very well, so I wanted a young child who had not yet started school.

I had very little real idea about disability, although I have a good friend who is disabled. I had ideas of a child with partial deafness or blindness, or with mobility problems and such like. The whole world of communication difficulties and other more complicated disabilities was almost completely unknown to me and I thought there were many disabilities that I wouldn't be able to cope with at all.

It took nine months between the time I enquired about adoption and the time I was approved to adopt. This was a real boost to my confidence after the long time of feeling low after the miscarriages.

I was immediately told about a child, 8 years of age, who had spina bifida. I saw her a few times and liked her a lot, but something told me it wouldn't work, so I didn't go through with that. Over the next year I was given information about three other children with different disabilities. Each time I prepared myself and imagined my life with that particular child, and each time I wasn't considered. It felt like a real loss on each occasion, but it gave me the time to think of the implications of different disabilities and how having any of those three children would change my life. Each time I moved on a little bit.

In the meantime, I went on a Special Needs Adopters' course where I met other people wanting to adopt special needs children. Most of them were married couples and wanted children over 5 years old, but I really enjoyed the course. I can't remember much of the content, except that we had lots of discussions about situations that might be presented to us, and what we would do. What I do remember is that we all had a common experience of loss around children. This included infertility, miscarriage, inherited disease in the family and children who had died. Having that experience in common with other people reaffirmed to me that I really was doing what I wanted to do.

I also went on a course for respite carers. I thought that if I was never able to have a child, I would like to do some respite care. I enjoyed that course a lot too and met some lovely people but felt that it wasn't for me at that time.

Then, about fourteen months after I had been approved to adopt, when time was going by very slowly and I thought nothing would ever happen, I was told about Maresa. She was then 18 months old, was said to have cerebral palsy and was living with a foster family. For the next six weeks, I had to see endless people – social workers, the doctor, the speech therapist, the physiotherapist and then the foster parents. It was only after I had seen and talked to all these people who were involved with Maresa that I was finally allowed to see her at the foster parents' home.

Becoming a parent

I still remember it. I was standing in the hallway and the foster mother was carrying Maresa downstairs. She was so beautiful, quite round and with dark curly hair and dark brown eyes. I sat holding her on the sofa for the next hour and she was smiling. The social worker and foster mother were both there and the foster mother invited me to come round on Sunday to spend a little time with her on my own. It was then Friday and I had been told by the social worker that I had to make up my mind by Monday whether I wanted to have her. The turmoil was enormous. I was still working, I hadn't organised an income for myself and yet I was being told that once I had made up my mind Maresa could move in within a few days.

I wanted her but I couldn't think how I was going to organise everything. Luckily, I had a friend staying in the house and she and another friend went through with me what I wanted to do and how I could do it. They made me able to be clear. I spent some time on Sunday morning with Maresa on my own and then talked with the foster mother about the best plan for the changeover.

We made a plan that would take about eight weeks. This was both for me, so that I could organise some leave from my job and make sure I had some income, and also for the foster parents who clearly needed time to say goodbye. In that time, I would see Maresa twice a week, so by the time she moved in she would know me a little.

Why did I decide to have Maresa when I had decided not to have other children I had been told about? The social worker who saw me when I was being approved once said that if it feels right, even if you don't know why, you just have to decide to jump into the unknown. I think that such instinctive feelings do have a lot to do with it but I also think that these feelings may be based on very rational reasons which are not verbalised at the time. I suppose I decided to trust my feelings. It was also important that the foster parents were very positive about Maresa and I trusted them too. They knew it would be difficult but they also knew Maresa's strengths, and were optimistic about things working well.

After the eight weeks we had planned I was just longing for Maresa to move in, and so, on October 17, 1986, she did. She was then 22 months old. I fostered her for ten months and the following September the adoption went through.

For me becoming a parent, a single parent, was not only a positive decision but something I had to work pretty hard to achieve. Once I had achieved it I was quite worried about how I would be. People talked about post adoption depression and I was trying to be prepared for everything. But as usual that's almost impossible.

Remembering

I remember Maresa's look of complete blankness that first weekend. She was clearly frightened and hadn't gone to sleep until the early hours of the morning. I was trying to do things like make shelves after she had gone to sleep. I remember that I found it difficult to stop doing other things. One problem of not having a pregnancy is that everything is so sudden. There is no gradual change or slowing down. In fact, it took me about eighteen months to slow down.

I remember that I just wanted to hold her all the time and not do anything else. Because of her disability, we had endless appointments with the physiotherapist, speech therapist, teacher, etc. and, although I wanted to know what to do to help her, I sometimes resented all the time that it took. I just wanted to lie in bed with her, play and go for walks with her.

I remember around our first Christmas feeling really starry eyed and in love and not wanting to to anything else except be with her.

In spite of all these feelings, I was still doing a lot of other things. I was going to meetings in the evenings, doing things around the house, painting walls, etc. so when Maresa had wakeful nights I hadn't adjusted to the fact that to be up several hours in the night meant that there were things I had to stop doing. The days that worked best were the ones with no other commitments, when sleeping when we needed to was a priority. At that time, I began to make some new friends, friends who were particularly interested in Maresa.

I went back to the practice nurse half of my job after the first three months. After having had some preliminary difficulties with childcare, a woman from the respite care scheme looked after Maresa for those two days. She was a real friend to me at that time.

As that first year went on and I was both getting to know Maresa and adjusting to my life as a parent, I found myself getting less interested in my work and the other outside things I was involved with. I don't know whether that was because, as a single parent, I couldn't just walk out and leave the situation for someone else to look after, or whether it was because I was becoming absorbed in my new life, or because I was just becoming tired. It was probably a combination of all these things. After I had had Maresa for about eighteen months I hurt my back and needed a lot of help for a few weeks. I decided then to have some more leave from work and during that time I worked out that, taking into account the benefits I could get, I could afford not to work. So I decided to leave my job permanently and I have never regretted that decision.

Full-time parenting

One thing I liked then and I still like about being a single parent is just being able to decide to do something or try something out, even if it turns out to be a mistake. I do sometimes think it would be wonderful to have someone who is as committed as I am to Maresa, to talk things over with, or to agonise with, but I have usually found somebody to do those things with, someone who has more distance from her and maybe can be just as helpful. I have usually found people I can enjoy her with too, which is just as important.

During that first year I did have some crises of confidence. At one time I felt that the endless visits to and by therapists were just undermining who I was and how I was as a mother, I didn't want to be just another of Maresa's therapists. Eventually, I was put in touch with another woman who had also adopted a child with a disability. Her situation was very different from mine but she recognised the problems I was experiencing and gave me an enormous amount of confidence in myself as a parent. I've rediscovered the wisdom of what she said over and over again – 'Listen to what they all say and then forget most of it'. She helped me to understand that a child needs a parent first and, as I see it, the job of the 'team' of speech therapists, physiotherapists, teachers etc., should be to give enough attention, information and access to resources, to enable a parent to give her child whatever is needed to help them get through the difficulties the disabilities bring. The therapists and teachers have information and resources that parents need and there should be a way of making these usable by parents or carers. In no way do such people know the child better and neither, in most circumstances, could they do a better job with the child than the parent.

Now, in our everyday life together, our good times are the times when Maresa and I are very much together, just sitting around not doing much, playing, going out, or spending time with people we both enjoy. The difficult times are when I want to do something and Maresa wants me to do something else with her, because it's difficult for her to play or get on with something of her own.

Sometimes I think it would be easier if there were other adults or older children in our household who enjoyed Maresa and could play endlessly with her. The reality is that if we were a family with others around that still might not happen. On the other hand, if it did, life might well be easier. I don't know. It would feel difficult now to give up the good times we have on our own, but again I suppose you can still have those too with other people around in the right way.

Disability

Having Maresa has made the issue of disability central in my life. I identify myself much more as a parent of a child with a disability than as a single parent. I get a lot of my support in the way of talking things over when I feel confused, or sharing things I feel excited about, from other parents of children with disabilities. It is they who know what I'm talking about, even if their children have different disabilities from Maresa's.

Housing and education in relation to disability are also very big things in my life now, and have been for the last three years, ever since I decided to move out of my terraced house. The house had become very difficult, mainly because when Maresa was 2 years old we were loaned an electric wheelchair. With three steps to the side door and five steps to the back door, it was almost impossible to get the wheelchair in and out of the back yard, which was where she wanted to use it most. The house had lots of small rooms and very steep stairs and so it had become quite impractical to continue living there. I felt it a lot at that time because it was about then that I hurt my back. It wasn't easy to decide what sort of housing was best. I was living in my own house so it seemed sensible to buy again, but how? Bungalows were impossibly expensive, and accessible flats with any sort of garden were very rare indeed in the area where we lived. So in the end, a friend, who was also a single parent, decided to buy a large house with me which we could make into two flats. It was a good idea, but after spending a lot of thought, energy and money it didn't work out.

Since I have had Maresa I've been in two situations living with other people and their children, and neither has worked, partly because living in close proximity to anyone else and her children is difficult, but also because having a disabled child does make for a different life style. The first year there was another woman and her son, who was the same age as Maresa, living in my house. At first I enjoyed having them there, and my friend was very helpful to me. But as time went on, I found it very difficult. Although we were living in the same house, we were two separate units. I was a very new parent and was learning about having to adjust to being flexible to Maresa's need to take time, to her patterns of eating, sleeping, waking up. I wanted to have control over how long we took to do these things. I suppose I couldn't cope with adjusting to yet more people's needs. Another factor was that I wanted to concentrate on being a new parent, whereas my friend was further on and wanted to work and go out.

The second house share, where we were in two flats in the big house, I thought would work well, but it didn't. Besides the usual things which make living with other people in close proximity difficult, there were the less obvious issues of disability. There we were, Maresa and I, in our lovely flat with everything accessible, but Maresa could hear games, and children playing upstairs, doing things that were quite out of her reach. So the feeling of being left out, rather than being intermittent, was nearly always there, unless children were actively doing something with her. So, although in theory we had control of our space, in practice we didn't because of the close proximity of a very different way of life.

Both times were an experiment and I don't think there will be any long-term regrets at the learning experiences. Maresa and I need other people around, but because of her particular needs, it has to be on our terms for at least some of the time. So it works better living on our own with regular time with other people.

Education too needs lot of thought. Maresa has now started school. It is a very nice school and I decided on it after having looked at a lot of schools. However, to find this school I have had to move to another city. Maresa, besides her physical difficulties, has communication difficulties and some learning difficulties. Since she went to nursery nearly three years ago, people have found her both difficult to assess and to get results from. She has a very astute awareness of people and an amazing sense of humour. Maybe there are many children, like Maresa, who have communication and learning difficulties, but who also have these other qualities. The more I think about all this, the more I find that I don't know what learning difficulties mean, except that some children are developing in a different way from the majority and need specific help. Also it is difficult to separate the fact that Maresa had three mothers in the first two years of her life, from her developmental problems and difficulty in settling into school.

So being an adoptive mother and a mother of a child with a disability are the central issues in my life with Maresa. To ignore the issue of disability seems to me now to be ignoring the most fundamental questions about what life is all about. To me, it can be liberating to have Maresa there, reminding me all the time that the most important things in life are not about achieving more and more, or acquiring more and more. The difficulties are those of a society that doesn't know how to listen, laugh, have fun and provide basic necessities for everyone. When I'm angry that is what I'm angry about. Maresa can have as much fun as anybody, but is more often excluded because people haven't the time to listen and play, or because places or things, such as swings in the playground, are inaccessible to her. I realise this when we've had a good time with people who can listen and play or we've found a good place where Maresa can take part.

How I have changed

When I think of myself four and a half years ago, I realise how much I have changed. I have slowed down. My view of 'success' has changed. I have learnt to look and listen in a different way. My values and what I think important have changed. I notice different things. I notice people more. I've always had a sense of humour but it's developing further.

The things that drive me most mad about Maresa are also the things that have changed me, and I like that. I love the way she likes me. I like her perceptiveness of me and the way she laughs at me, especially when I start shouting at the wall.

I find her 'I won't' very difficult, but it makes me think, and how else can she make me think? She can't talk. Her frustration and withdrawal upset me, but again push me to wonder what she is finding difficult in her life. How else is she to make her feelings felt? So I have slowed down and begun to listen with my whole self. All this needs a lot of time. Breakfast can take an hour but it's well worth the time. As a result of all this I have stopped work, and my evening commitments got dropped one by one. I've started to read more. When I first had Maresa there seemed to be not enough time to just sit and think and it felt like being deprived of something essential. I am now able to do this and I have started to think about what new things I would like to learn about and do.

Although we still do have difficult times, and thinking about Maresa's everyday needs and how I can get them met still takes an enormous amount of thought, time and energy, I also feel that my life is very exciting. I love Maresa's courage and striving to be herself, however difficult that may be. I love the way she likes people and wants to be with them, how she enjoys the rough sea, the woods, or a dog wanting to play. I love her excitement, playfulness and sense of humour.

BYGONE ILLUSIONS AND BEGOTTEN CONTRADICTIONS

KATE MARIAT

The decision to leave became firmly established in my mind over a period of about a week. There was no alternative. He must have sensed my resolution and with tacit stubborness remained in the house for days, watching and waiting. I managed to slip out one afternoon to a phone box. I couldn't be sure when we could get away but that didn't seem to matter, we had somewhere to go. He slept downstairs – as if we would slip out in the night. It was a silent contest of wills. One of these tense nights I had a dream set in arcadian meadows and knew as I awoke that I must take the children with me, that it was somehow necessary for their survival too. But for this dream I might have succumbed to the pressure and escaped on my own.

Achieving single parenthood

About a week later I had the opportunity to pick up the bag of nappies that had lain subversively waiting for days, get myself and my two daughters out of the house and to the station, without being seen by anyone we knew. Two short train rides, a phone call and a lift later, we arrived at a recently established Women's Aid refuge. I felt the first rush of relief as the train pulled out of the station with us safely aboard. The second came as we entered the refuge, anonymous, and with an awakening sense of control derived from the knowledge that no one need know where we were, unless I chose to say. It was a new start for us all and was, for me, a decisive first step towards making a life that I wanted. I didn't realise then what a long struggle I had initiated in claiming my life for myself and even now, with my daughters in their teens, I am not sure how far I have come.

Over the next weeks the problems were essentially practical, tractable and thankfully preoccupying: interviews with the DHSS, solicitors and local infants school, seeking an injunction, petitioning for a divorce and, most of all, maintaining secrecy. The latter was instinctively prioritised and rightly so; months later I discovered just how extensive the enquiries he had made about us had been. My gaping wounds and inarticulate questions – why had I needed to leave, what had happened, was I justified and on what basis – were tightly bandaged and tucked away, only to be unravelled in small, manageable insights over many years. It really was survival. At some barely conscious level I was determined not to become my mother – stifled, derided, undermined – a martyr to her sense of duty and respectability, her guilt. Yet in many ways I am her.

Parenting at the refuge was of necessity basic and revolved around food – instant everything, especially mash. Communal living dissipated the intensity of parental responsibility, or perhaps it was the company that made it lighter work. The routine went: feed them, school them, out to play (the refuge had a large walled garden), then bed. Our own lives rallied over tea and cigarettes, usually round the enormous kitchen table, where exchanges of shared experience provided validation and reassurance. Despite frequent traumatic eruptions – usual in any crowded living situation – the refuge did provide much needed security. I did not fully appreciate this until after returning home, where vulnerability and isolation reigned supreme.

I'd never wanted to marry. I'd got pregnant, had insufficient courage for an abortion and allowed myself to be cornered. But I liked the idea of having a child in total ignorance of the reality. My mother had told me time and again during my childhood, 'Oh I wouldn't have children if I were you.' Yet when I confirmed her suspicions of pregnancy, she replied, 'Oh but you'll love it so much', a response that surprised me in the light of her advice. I didn't know what I'd feel, I only knew that my reality of barren aspirations was bound to change.

It never occurred to me to have a child and not bring it up; I believe that mothers are important. I remember having a heated argument with one of the women who regularly volunteered at the refuge, when she questioned the necessity of mothers, my first encounter with such a notion. Then, I thought she was daft – wasn't the necessity staring her in the face? Now, I would emphasise the quality of a child/adult relationship rather than biological tie. But few non-mothers are prepared to make the commitment, take the responsibility that childcare requires, even part-time, and who can blame them? When it came to it, I didn't want anyone elso to bring my daughters up, but then no acceptable alternative was on offer. In retrospect, even an occasional reliable and trusted co-parent would have brought welcome relief.

An eye-opening encounter with the official attitude to divorcing women came in the magistrates' court at the hearing for my injunction. My soon-to-be-ex-husband arrived, complete with moral support, to request access to the children. I had naïvely hoped my affidavit would forestall access. I asked my solicitor to object on the grounds that the children had been through a lot of upheaval and I wanted time to settle them down before access began. The magistrate replied 'I've heard that one before', and, while granting the injunction, ordered access every Saturday and a welfare report. His presumption that I was not concerned with the children's needs left me stunned – were divorcing women bad mothers? My (male) solicitors had not warned me this could happen. I only wanted the house back for us to be left alone. They had a monopoly on refuge custom and pushing through injunctions was making them a good living. I had not been advised of the advantages of waiting a while before requesting a court hearing. Legal action was what I wanted because it was decisive, but then I had a misguided belief in justice.

Returning to the vacated house, was for me, like walking back into a cell after the door had been opened, but the children were delighted and at least now there was potential for a better life. In the heat of the 1976 summer the house stank; just about everything was either filthy or mouldy. He had neglected to take most of his possessions, even to flush the toilet and had left irritating little notes under various pillows. We arrived on a Friday evening to a ringing phone; the first access visit was to be the next day.

Once the house was thoroughly cleaned and his belongings dispatched, I asked the council to transfer the tenancy to my name. They refused until after the divorce. An interim maintenance hearing, prescribed by my solicitors against my wishes was – thankfully – dismissed. The magistrate said we were all right on the social, and we were. The money was regular, more than we were used to, and represented the negation of one major source of hassle. A period of abeyance followed when I was informed I would have to fight for custody, a daunting prospect. I perceived surreptitious forms of pressure – ranging from a break-in to gifts, subtle taunts, phone calls to seduction – injunction no deterrent. I instructed my solicitor to proceed with the case; he withdrew.

Early in 1977, the divorce hearing lasted about five minutes and that evening two women friends took me out to celebrate my autonomous parenthood. I was optimistic about my life with my daughters. I didn't realise then that what I had just achieved was the easy bit.

In pursuit of autonomy

And so, with my mantle of optimism I got down to the serious task of parenting – the sheer delight of being able to take charge, structure, regulate and cohere our lives. Having reorganised our living space we began to have proper meals at fairly regular intervals and my elder daughter, who had always refused anything that wasn't chips, egg yolk, marmite crackers or sweets, began to extend her range a bit. We went on walks and picnics to the river or the woods and collected kindling wood. We went on a day trip to Brighton when not even my younger daughter's 'banana sick' on the coach spoiled our enjoyment – we washed our clothes in the sea. We even managed three days at a B & B in Dorset and, having to be off the premises during the day, found ourselves walking cheerfully along the beach in the rain.

I made no effort to maintain previous acquaintances, taking the view that we were safest with the fewest number of access routes he could have to us as possible. (I assumed he would try and get at us – not so much physically as emotionally – and he did.) They soon dropped away, including two women friends with whom I would have liked to have kept in touch. I found out much later that he had had relationships – of sorts – with both of them and that each had had a child by him. Years later one of them got in touch again and although we rarely see each other, she remains a very special friend; the only friend I have who can make that part of my past real.

Initially I had wanted to get a council house exchange and move as soon and as far away as possible – to make the new start absolute. However, when, after advertising, I was actually offered an exchange in Cornwall, I could not bring myself to take it. Partly it felt like running away and, though the urge to do so was very strong, an intrinsic part of me felt the only way to resolve the difficulties was to stay and face them. I also felt we would be even more vulnerable in a strange place. At least tucked away in the corner of our council estate, the neighbours were always alert to anything extraordinary. I began to realise the impossibility of dispensing with our past, even if I had changed our future. My daughters' responses to reading this paragraph are illuminating. My elder daughter affirmed 'Yes, it would have been easier if we'd moved, we would have been better off in a city.' My younger daughter ruminated, 'Yes . . . I know what you mean . . . it's like when I started [her present] school . . . I'm glad I stayed . . . it sort of makes you stronger having coped.' And they are both right.

The main difficulties over this period seemed to revolve around the access visits, from which the children often returned fractious, overwrought and wilful. Sometimes it would take two or three days to restore equilibrium, leaving three or four days before the next round. I came to the conclusion that it was not so much his daughters he cared for, as his own feelings – inextricably bound up with pride. I was also open to the possibility that there was a bit of subtle manipulation going on, but only now, since talking to my elder daughter in the course of writing this, can I affirm that there was. Then, I had only my suspicions and felt I could do nothing without some confirmation. Dealing with this was stressful and I needed support.

When one morning before school my elder daughter, by then six, said she was going to kill herself, I ignored it. When this challenge was repeated on a subsequent morning, I told her she'd better hurry up and do it or we'd be late for school. The bluff worked but her bid for special attention was effective. I asked her teacher how she thought my daughter was and explained that the access visits were causing problems. Even though she had been in school for over a year she couldn't read. The teacher was taking a 'She'll come to it when she's ready' approach, bestowing on her an extended reception period. The school was very middle class and at that time there was no other child in a similar situation. Today my daughter can recall with a wry smile the way she heard herself whispered about by some of the mothers – 'parents divorced, mother hasn't got much money – you know' – and how she was taunted by another girl. I had apparently taken her to the doctor on such an occasion thinking she was ill; only now can she tell me that she had no way of communicating her distress at this ostracism. Her teacher gave her an IQ test and because her score was high – whatever that means – it was decided that she was 'disturbed'. By some procedure I can't remember she was, or rather all of us were, given an appointment at the child guidance clinic. As the appointments were held during school hours, her withdrawal from the classroom made her feel even more different.

The child guidance clinic was like a trial without a charge. I simply had to interact with my children and answer the odd question, while one 'magistrate' made copious notes and the other observed our every move. It was an intimidating set up. I explained about the access difficulties (being at the time unaware of the precise nature of the school situation) but they were quite dismissive. Perhaps the problem was me. The imposition of this unspoken doubt was unnecessary and caused additional stress at a time when I needed support. I withdrew us from further appointments, though I suspect that some contact between clinic and school was maintained for a while. I talked to my mother about the situation. She suggested that I try and give my elder daughter some time on her own with me each day, which I did. I also initiated a 'happy day' routine. Each day was started anew with cheery delight, breakfast became a feast – porridge or boiled eggs on alternate mornings. The effort mustered, I almost came to believe in it myself. I had total responsibility and was held totally responsible, but had autonomy only in domestic matters.

The situation was finally resolved by a combination of changed circumstances. Later, in 1977, I became one of a group of mothers who sought to set up a playgroup in an empty room in the school. By coincidence, the woman eventually employed to run it was the mother of an old friend who, during the short time that she worked there, gave me a lot of support. She persuaded me to apply to college and after an exchange of letters with the college authorities and two interviews, I was offered a place. My mother agreed to have the children after school and playgroup (there was only one childminder in the area and she never had a free place) and so I accepted, dismissing any doubts that my mother, glad to be rid of her own childrearing responsibilities, may have had reservations.

From the time I got the college place, I began to notice subtle differences in my daughter's teachers' attitudes towards me. They began to address me slightly differently, explain things as though I would understand, tell me things I was sure they would not have told me before. Looking back, I am sure they were not conscious of this change; they were sincere and well-intentioned women. But if they were treating me differently, then perhaps their expectations of my daughter had also changed. Soon after I started college in October 1978, I cut off the access visits. I cannot remember what prompted this action, but, until December (when I was summoned to court for new access arrangements and at my request, a supervision order), the children did have two settled months. By the end of this time my elder daughter could read. The access visits began to improve after the break, though they remained a source of tension. In practice the supervision was nominal, but the existence of the order seemed sufficient for their father to feel monitored. The succession of social workers sent to visit us every six months had little insight into the situation and I sometimes wondered just who was being supervised. By the time I was informed, some years later, that the order had been lifted, I had long discarded it as a potential source of support.

During those first two years, before I went to college, I was utterly immersed in the mother role, totally preoccupied with day to day coping. I barely noticed that my needs – social, emotional, sexual – went completely unmet, nor, if I got round to thinking about it at all, could I see any way to meet them. I felt under pressure from all sides to be an exemplary mother (a pressure I had not experienced within the respectability of a destructive marriage) and I knew our survival depended on my compliance. A quiet cup of tea and a cigarette during odd hours when the children were out playing, represented a pinnacle of indulgence, something I could claim for myself and as such, was reliable, regular and not be underestimated. My need for escapism was to some extent met by excursions to the library and a correspondence course in astrology which gave my mind endless maze-like paths to wander. In this remote exile of others' expectations, it felt as though my self as a distinct entity barely existed, even for me, let alone anyone else. Yet it did exist and hallmarked everything I did.

One thing that would have made a difference over this period would have been a really good friend. I had made new acquaintances – loose ties tethered by the mother role – all but one married, though from that one I learnt a lot about fighting back. The cost of coping burst out periodically in all sorts of physical symptoms, real and imagined: in fear – of threats, of others' expectations, of being ill, of what will happen to the children if something happens to me. The price was very high. Now, it is difficult to recall the intensity of those bleak washes of anxiety. Then, it was a condition of life. And for the most part a hidden condition; others saw only my strength.

Despite what seem now to have been intolerable constraints and isolation, within those confines it was a positive time. I gradually redecorated the house, made bread, grew vegetables, fruit and even wheat in the garden, read to the children most nights and with them, took satisfaction and delight in small everyday things. We were better off. Over our second winter I had the worst depression I had then experienced. It was caused by the feeling of having reached an impasse; optimism and determination were not enough. The access situation at that time felt like a noose. No matter how much effort I made in our domestic lives my achievements could always be undermined. And one very bleak night I can remember sitting by the fire after the children had gone to bed and from underneath all the exhaustion and necessity, the thin trickle of a need leaked out – 'I want some fun.' But I was in no position to claim it.

The depression passed, circumstances changed and I remember the months before I started college as one of the most contented periods of my life. I had a future of my own.

A confident dependency

College work kept me busy and I discovered not only that I could do the work, but that I could do it quite well. In this respect, education provided me with a sense of self-worth previously unknown. I acquired a provisional confidence. My feelings about this form of institutional validation are now more ambivalent. Certainly I needed it – as did my daughters at school – and certainly education was a positive experience for me. (I was lucky. I had good teachers and 'fitted into' the department of my chosen subject – art.) But this re-evaluation also created a dependency. My self-esteem was achieved by means of others' judgments of my worth – the novelty of approval. Only now, after having rejected my education and my job, am I thinking about how to value who I am and what I can do on my own terms, while retrieving what I learnt from both experiences.

Then, I became dimly aware that my education was intricately bound up with our survival, in terms of being listened to, taken seriously – the respect it attracted. Our autonomy as a family slowly increased with the respectability my education bestowed. We became less vulnerable primarily as a result of people's changing attitudes towards us – our changing status. In respect of the professionals with whom we had to deal, it was like joining a club and I used it, without considering the ethics of the process, or the assumptions that had given rise to our negative image. As my elder daughter accurately observed after reading this paragraph, 'If you hadn't gone to college me and [her sister] probably wouldn't be taking our exams.' It even seems feasible to ask if she would have learnt to read. My education not only offered us confidence in our own abilities, it also allowed my daughters to be seen as potentially capable – they could be expected to achieve.

The amount of time I spent at college contracted my parenting time significantly. We could become separate beings and our relationship with each other became in many ways more respectful, more enjoyable. Parenting became less of a burden. My daughters' recollections of my college years range from raspberry picking in the garden for 5p a cup, to soapy topknots on bath nights and white items of washing regularly, to their annoyance, turning out various shades of pink. They remember half-terms spent making pots in the ceramics studio, summers camping in the New Forest till the money ran out and, in winter, negotiating turns on the highly prized territory of the black rug in front of the fire. This was where, on Sundays, baked potatoes and hard brussels sprouts were wheeled in on a squeaky trolley, some weeks the only meal we ate together. These were pleasures. I can also remember their emotional demands and my efforts to keep firm the boundaries of acceptable behaviour they inevitably pushed against. I learnt how to outwit manipulations and found autocracy an effective way of maintaining all our equilibriums, They have reminded me of one occasion when, at the end of my tether and in order to put a stop to a squalling squabble, I threatened to bang their heads together. Being familiar with this particular threat they didn't think I'd do it. The resulting knock effectively coerced them into bed in stunned silence.

Our strength as a family grew with our increasing independence as individuals. I began to find it easier to make clear the boundaries of my tolerance and this too contributed to making us all more secure. Nevertheless, my sense of our vulnerability took many years to fade. A recurrent nagging apprehension probably inhibited my daughters' initiative, not because they weren't responsible, but because I sensed a precariousness in our new-found stability. They were 10 and nearly 7 years old before I allowed them to come home from school on their own.

And still I had no social life. On rare occasions I went out, usually for something dutiful like a meeting, but even when the outing was nominally social, I often ended up feeling vaguely inane – disengaged. My daughters might have liked it if I had gone out more often. They informed me when they no longer needed a babysitter, but part of the bargain was that I should pay them instead – responsibility money for looking after themselves. Now, it is painful to recollect the chasm that existed between the social interaction available to me and my self. Then, I liked to think I was self-sufficient and was certainly seen as such by others. It wasn't what I wanted; the emotional isolation was profound.

It was while I was at college that I first found myself attracted to a woman in a consciously sexual way. There had been other women I'd mysteriously longed to be close to; this pervasive eroticisim was different and entirely compelling. But if I wanted, needed a lover, I could see no practical way to fit one into my life. Fully aware of my desires, I had no idea how to be open about them – let alone the confidence – and felt, all considered, I was in no position to try. So I basked in her company whenever I could and there were times when she went out of her way to do things for me. I was unable even to reciprocate her tentative interest in me. I longed for some eventuality that would resolve the situation, but of course it never happened; I gave her no indication of how I felt. It never occurred to me to define these feelings as lesbian, let alone myself as such, anymore than I thought of myself as a mother. There was a gap between the fact that I had and was bringing up children, and what I felt to be me; mothering was what I *did*. I tacitly acknowledged that I could be attracted to a woman and that (at some stage) this was what I wanted, then tucked this information away – a potential given life only in dreams and fantasy. It took some years to emerge as a reality.

By 1983, I was in my first year of teaching, still studying and trying to make use of rented studio space nine miles away via public transport. I had chosen to teach part-time in order to continue art making, which had become an essential means of exploring and defining my experience. I had been offered the only job I (hesitantly) applied for – in a sixth-form college – but while teaching remained a sensible choice in respect of my daughters, what I wanted was some scope for fulfilment. I threw myself into all the work, but gradually realised I simply couldn't do it all. I could not maintain this life of my own at the level of absorption both it and I required, and teach, and still have time for my daughters. Even with the relief of what had become (temporarily) regular and reliable weekend access visits, I began to feel stretched – under pressure. It was as if I had been offered a telescope with which to survey new horizons, while overlooking the chasm of parental responsibility at my feet.

By the end of the year I had finished studying and given up the studio, but without these activities to provide a sense of meaning and the (idealistic) hope of more interesting work, I was left with the disillusion of a stifling job and the fractious intrigue of departmental politics. With nothing to strive for and no means of affirmation, my confidence began to dissipate. I found it difficult to maintain a sense of my own worth outside the context that had awarded it. However, the conflict between what I wanted for myself and my daughters' needs remained. It has since been compromised but not resolved.

My education had lifted us out of inconsequence (if not relative poverty), but it had also given me expectations, enabled me to develop abilities and interests – needs – that were not, in terms of employment or my circusmstances, going to be easy to satisfy.

Facing up to conflicts

Having been lucky enough to get a teaching job at a time when such jobs were scarce, to some extent I resigned myself to it. I had supposed that the job would be relatively interesting, but found that the constraints of the examination system and the dictates of a rigid departmental organisation left little room for stimulating work. With, as far as I could see, no hope of improving the situation, my dissatisfaction grew. An accumulation of submerged boredom and frustration served to make the job a repository for much that was wrong with my life, including my isolation. I soon began to feel stuck, trapped. I wanted to leave, but felt wary of discarding the protection of respectability that the job bestowed on us. For my daughters (the elder by then in the lower years of secondary school, the younger in the upper years of junior school) this period was one of confident stability – a notably happy and settled time. I did not realise just how happy they were until I talked to them in the course of writing this. They remember me as particularly strong when I was teaching. This discrepancy between how they saw me and how I felt about what I was doing was one of the many contradictions of the period.

There were also contradictions in my position at the college. An ex-grammer school maintaining the traditions of a public school, the atmosphere was one of privilege. There were rarely any students from the council estate where we lived. I was disturbed to discover that some of the teachers employed women to clean their homes – the kind of work I'd needed to go out and do before my younger daughter was born. I was and wasn't one of them. I didn't want to be one of them. I buried my ambivalence. During a series of half-day teachers' strikes, I felt the incongruity of striking alongside people, some of whom earned twice my salary and others whose incomes made up less than half that of their households. It was not so much that I minded about the money – though I could have done with more. Then, as now, I valued my time more than money. It was rather that the financial disparity behind the unity of industrial action heightened my disaffection. Such contradictions also played a part in the erosion of my confidence.

Now, I can wonder if I would have found the job less thwarting if I'd been happier, if perhaps I could have laughed more easily at the absurdities of the system and my position in it. Then, I found myself in a position that was affirmative for my daughters, but becoming intensely difficult for me. In the absence of other sources of fulfilment, I needed my work to be reasonably satisfying. My life with my daughters was satisfying, but, while it consumed much of my existence, it engaged only a part of me. I had never wanted parenting to be more than part of my life – it would not have been good for my daughters if I had – but increasingly I had to acknowledge the extent to which my needs were not being met. I wasn't even sure what they were. I was aware of needs for my daughters' well-being and my own (by then beleaguered) fulfilment, but it was beyond me then to define the absence of meaningful communication in my life – the need for intimacy, passion, for adventure. I was finally induced to face up to my isolation by the successive, if disparate, developments of getting to know another lesbian and my daughters' father going to prison. These two events, conflated by time, marked a turning point.

It wasn't the first time their father had found himself on the wrong side of the law. Some years earlier, the local paper had reported that part of his plea in a court case had been that his wife had left him. I'd been mildly amused by such a disingenuous excuse. He'd also told the court that the fine imposed would prevent him from taking his daughters on holiday. I'd been annoyed at the ease with which he linked us to him. In another case, he'd made such a complex sham of his defence that the report had taken up half a page of the newspaper. I'd been angry at his self-interested oblivion to the distress (acute in the case of my elder daughter) that the report would cause his daughters, living in a small town as we did then. By the time he went to prison they were more secure, less vulnerable, and this time the local paper did not catch up with the story. They were distressed, but their concern was for their father to whom they displayed a stoic, if cautious, loyalty.

It was the same loyalty they showed to me when I told them I was a lesbian, in their eyes then no lesser shame and embarrassment and one more attestation to their 'oddity.' For me, the positive acknowledgment of my sexuality was reassuring, a confirmation of an essential part of my self, It was like stepping into a new life and I began to make some of the best friends I've ever had. It also introduced me to new conflicts, not least those between the demands of relationships and parenting.

Only now am I coming to realise the disparity between my own and my daughters' experience of this period. It was a positive and expansive time for me, but a tense and stressful one for them.

My daughters' experience of their father's imprisonment was confined by secrecy. He'd been remanded a day before he was due to take them on holiday, so they went to stay with his mother for a week instead. In talking to my younger daughter recently about how she felt at that time, she said she knew something was going on, but that no one told her anything. She remembers her sister going out with her father's girlfriend (to visit him) and asking if she could go too. Then, having been told that she couldn't, asking where they were going and not being told. (She was 10 at the time.) Later, her sister told her where they'd been. She thought I'd withheld the information from her – as her grandmother had – because she was 'too young' and was justifiably resentful of this. I thought I'd told her when I told her sister, the same day I was told. I obviously (and inexcusably) didn't. It wasn't deliberate; she must have been out playing while I was preoccupied with my own unsettled plans. Once she knew, she was able to go and visit him too.

Their father was away for six months. I could and did relax. The sense of relief was unexpected and immense. I began to realise the extent to which his existence had caused me apprehension, recognise by its absence a constant feeling that, given the opportunity, he would destablise us. I could drop my guard, a guard I wasn't aware of having developed until I didn't need it. I could acknowledge these deeply buried fears as the source of my sense of our vulnerability and how much I had censored our lives because of them. I realised I'd felt that living our lives, in particular my life, in a way that was beyond reproach, would somehow deny him the opportunity to intervene. Looking back this was true, but paradoxically, this realisation released me from the pressures of respectability. The effects were decisive. Firstly, as sex with a woman became a real possibility, I began, very slowly, to reorientate my life towards meeting my sexual needs. In so doing, I began to think seriously about my sexuality, though it was some years before I felt confident in my sexual identity. Secondly, my job became less important. The following year, after having worked for four years with progressively less commitment, I left. I now realise this was premature; it still meant a great deal to my daughters to be able to say 'my mum's a teacher'. I felt we were secure enough for me to begin to let go, just a little bit, though it had taken a decade to get there. It was the beginning of a long period of re-evaluation.

My sexuality was initially quite difficult for my daughters to come to terms with, not because they minded, but because they thought other people would. They didn't want anyone to know. At school, they began to experience the usual run of anti-gay jokes and jibes on a personal level. My elder daughter felt totally unable to tackle them, because she feared persecution that she would not be able to deal with. My younger daughter could not associate me, or other lesbians she had come to know and like, with the hatred and dismissal of lesbians she encountered at school and play. I can remember a peculiar conversation with her when she was in her first year at secondary school. She came in from playing and found me upstairs sorting clothes. 'I don't like lesbians.' 'I'm a lesbian.' 'I don't like lesbians.' But you like [I named some friends].' 'Ye-es,' she paused. 'I don't like lesbians.' And she went back out to play. When she read this passage we discussed whether or not I should include it. Sensitive though we both are to it, it illustrates an important point. It was not that she didn't like lesbians, it was what other people thought of lesbians that made her feel bad. She could not at that time reconcile their derision with her own experience.

There were other tensions too. When, for example, a lover became a frequent member of the household for a few months, my younger daughter enjoyed the extra attention, while my elder daughter showed signs of jealousy. It had not occurred to me the extent to which, as the elder one, she felt she had a prior claim to me. On reading this, she said it was because I hadn't consulted them about someone spending so much time with us. It also inhibited her social life. Her anxiety about the nature of the relationship being discovered prevented her from inviting her own friends to stay. Yet she didn't have any problem sharing me with my friends, even though they often stayed at the house and it was (and is) with my closest friends that I have my primary emotional relationships.

As some of my needs began to be met, others surfaced and I began to resent the restrictions of parental responsibility. My restlessness reached a peak in the winter of 1986–87 when, had acceptable alternative care been available for my daughters, I might have considered leaving. I doubt now whether I could have left and I am certainly glad that I didn't. My daughters were old enough to accept this urge for 'freedom', but at a cost. They began to feel they were tying me down. It took some time to reassure them that they were not personally responsible for my conflict, that it was caused by accumulated pressures, tensions – loneliness. I needed some fun. Over this period our (very elastic) family ties were stretched quite far, further than they had been before, or perhaps have been since.

For a year or two, my daughters experienced my sexuality as one more complication in their lives. As they got older, each found her own ways of coping with the prejudice. Moving to a city helped. My elder daughter found an ally in her best friend when her mother also came out as a lesbian and, later, in acquaintances who had gay brothers, lesbian sisters. She began to feel less vulnerable through establishing openness and finding acceptance. She says the biggest cause of difficulty she experienced at this time was living in a woman-only household. This was something her friends would not accept. She wanted men in her life. I respected her choice but didn't want them in the house. She wanted to bring them home. This conflict brewed for about a year; I have no regrets about my refusal to compromise. Eventually, when she was 18, she decided to move out, which was a relief for both of us. Looking back, I think we both used this issue to achieve a necessary break; eighteen years is quite long enough to live with a parent, or a child. Her independence has enabled our relationship to grow; we get on really well now. My younger daughter has been more circumspect in her adaption. She hasn't (yet) told any of her friends I'm a lesbian, a risk her self-containment does not predispose her to take. That it is a risk is the injustice.

My elder daughter said to me recently, 'At first I thought I was odd because we were poor, then I thought I was odd because you were a lesbian and now I think I'm just odd. I like being odd. I like being myself. I don't want to be anyone else.' Maybe contradictions beget insights. Both my daughters now see this strand of their experience as an important contribution to their understanding. They see their childhood, without denying its difficulties, as a positive contribution to who they are.

Growing up

My daughters are 19 and 16 years old now, and only in writing this have I come to realise how autonomous we've each become. I'm no longer bound by the umbilical cord of their need for support – my need to give it. I no longer feel indispensable. I don't worry about them as much as I used to. I have confidence in their growing ability to make their own lives. In less than two years my younger daughter will be leaving home and my life will be truly my own. The life I want for myself is not compatible with parenting.

I sometimes wonder who, where, I would be if I hadn't brought my daughters up – not me, not here. They have shaped my life as much as I theirs. They have given as much as they have taken and I have grown with and through them. I am certain this exchange was only possible *because* I was bringing them up on my own. Our relationships with each other have been positively formative for all of us. It could have been easier, though, with practical support for me rather than the pressures of the mother role, without the imposition of 'father right'. In retrospect, it's probably better that they've known their father, had a chance to make up their own minds. They are fond of him but have no illusions about him or what our lives would have been like if he had been part of our household. It may be their realism that, as they've grown up, has allowed their relationship with him to stabilise. Our separation from him was a prerequisite for what each of us has achieved – in terms of education, relationships and, most important, self-respect.

To say I have no regrets suggests choice. I wanted to bring my daughters up, yet there was no acceptable alternative. I needed to make a life for myself, yet it was (at least in part) having my daughters to strive for that enabled me to search for it, while my responsibilities for them held me back as I began to know what I wanted. But without them, perhaps I would not have found the life I now want to make.

A NINETEEN-PARENT FAMILY

MICHELINE MASON

To understand my viewpoint on parenting, you must first of all understand how my head got stuffed with nonsense in the first place.

My family was extremely normal: the 'right' height, the 'right' colour, the 'right' sort of intellect and generally nice people. My parents married at the 'right' age, and had a nice little able-bodied daughter. It was only when I was born that this near fairy-tale family life got all upset.

After just a few days of mistakenly thinking that their second daughter was just like any other 'normal' baby, my family realised that I was not fairy-tale stuff at all. I cried every time I was picked up or had my nappy changed, not just a little cry but a great big purple-faced scream. My horrified mother took me back to the hospital and asked if something was wrong. X-rays revealed two leg fractures, and a diagnosis of brittle bones (Osteogenesis Imperfecta) was made.

The condition was not very well understood in the 1950s, and my family received a lot of scare-mongering information. They were told that I would surely die quite soon, and should be christened in hospital as a matter of urgency. Obviously the doctors were wrong about many of their gloomy prophesies, but the damage to our relationship had been done.

My parents' initial delight in my birth turned to fear, disappointment and bewilderment, although I do believe I was always loved. I believe that even as a small baby I was aware of all these emotions, but decided that I had enough going for me to make the effort to survive.

My mother and father, like so many other people, had very little experience of disability or of disabled people. They believed most of what they were told, at first anyway. They were told that I would always be severely 'handicapped'. That I would become increasingly deformed as a result of numerous fractures. That I would always be dependent on them, and that I would be wanted only by them.

My early childhood was spent mostly in hospital where my cot was always labelled 'Minimal Handling'. This was a warning to the nurses not to try and pick me up, even if I was crying, in order to prevent accidental injury. The result for me was deprivation of the most essential healing power people can offer each other – a loving touch when it hurts. Luckily I did go home sometimes and, as my parents' confidence increased, they learnt that gentle and thoughtful handling was fine and that perhaps I was not as brittle as everyone feared.

They were, however, sufficiently scared and protective to agree with the education authorities that I was too fragile to go to school and so, when the time came, I was allocated Home Tuition. Consequently my education was conducted in solitary confinement, the ultimate in segregation.

I was considered bright, funny and a terrible shame.

My physical appearance, especially my very small stature, was talked about in hushed tones. 'Well at least she has a nice personality . . .' Even those features which were in no way affected by brittle bones were defined by my condition. My hair, for example, was seen as lovely but completely wasted on someone like me.

In retrospect I think it is quite amazing, although I did not realise it at the time, that in the whole of my childhood I can only remember one reference to my future adult life. This was a conversation between myself, my sister then aged about 12, and my mother. I cannot remember the origins of the subject, but a remark was made about my sister becoming an aunty. Her response was, 'Oh yes, and *who* is going to make me an aunty?' My mother said 'Ssssh!' and that was it – that was the only time my future adult life was ever referred to.

I was not told by my immediate family about menstruation even when it happened. I think, in fact, that they were quite surprised that it did happen. I had already found out all about it at the age of 10 from my cousin, and had lived very anxiously ever since, worrying that my body was too small to get the message that I was growing up. I was greatly relieved when it all started just as it should.

At the age of 14, I begged to be allowed to accept an opportunity which arose to go away to boarding-school. I felt that I was suffocating at home and going away seemed like an escape from death by boredom. It may well have been.

So I went to Florence Treloars Grammar School for Physically Disabled Girls. It was the first of its kind in Britain and I was one of only forty young women who came as pioneer pupils. It was wonderful to discover at last that there were other minds with ideas different to those of my family. I had an opportunity at last to talk about my doubts and insecurities, and to share my struggles to retain a self-image that was positive and hopeful. We laughed a lot about the funniness of the 'able-bodied'. (They did not appreciate this!)

Our academic abilities were nurtured very well compared to our previous experiences of so-called 'Special Education', but even here was the unspoken expectation that work would be 'instead of' the usual expectations of women – not only to work but also to get married and have a family. Our sexuality was barely acknowledged by the staff. We did not have any sex education. (This is no longer true at Treloars.) Amongst ourselves, of course, it was an OBSESSION!

The first adult who ever directly spoke to me about my own ability to have children was a doctor. I was 25. She was doing some research on Osteogenesis Imperfecta and I had agreed to be one of her subjects. I had agreed because she was a geneticist.

The thing was, you see, that deep down inside of me, I always believed that I was someone else. Not this shrunken, ugly invalid child with no hope except to sublimate my passions through Art, shut up at home, for the rest of my isolated little life. I believed that I was a tiny, compressed butterfly, ready to fly. I had then, as I do now, a haunting sense of mistaken identity. 'No! No! This is not me you see! This is your image of me plastered over your own eyes, distorting your view. *I* am over here! Look another way!'

This other compressed person had wisely chosen not to speak or ask questions of the confused adults around her. She only emerged in the quiet, lonely, dark hours of the night to dream about living a life full of experience, not observation. And that included the experience of parenting.

An angel plopped down from heaven

I was 32 when it happened. The pregnancy was not consciously planned, being conceived greatly against the odds whilst using contraceptives. Events from then on just overwhelmed me, and still do to this day. I feel as though I have been in a perpetual state of crisis, begun by having to make the decision of whether or not to continue with the pregnancy, and continued by voting 'Yes'. So I have been overwhelmed by my own choice. I want to take full credit for that. It did take courage, because I did not even know if I could physically survive a pregnancy, or if the baby would inherit my condition. Once I had made the decision to choose life, and whatever that may bring, the confirmation that the baby did indeed have brittle bones only seemed to make the initial decision more meaningful and special. When Lucy was finally born by caesarean section, I remember looking out of the window of St Thomas's Hospital at Big Ben, and thinking that it should have been on the ten o'clock news, it seemed so momentous to me. I had this wonderful sense of triumph. I had done it! I had proven both to myself and other people that my 'fragile' body was capable of the miracle of creating a new life. All its shortcomings seemed insignificant in comparison.

This larger-than-life feeling was exacerbated by the fact that, after I had been waiting in hospital for seven boring weeks before the birth, it seemed that everyone who worked there wanted to see my baby. When a commotion could be heard approaching in the corridor, I knew it was Lucy in her mobile incubator followed by a Special Care Unit Nurse, a Nursery Nurse, half the hospital's domestic staff and several patients. The breast-feeding advisor tried to clear the crowds around my bed, but the curtain kept popping open nevertheless. I was given a private room in the end. Despite this well-meant enthusiasm, I could not wait to get home, because I could not really believe that Lucy was real in that unreal setting. I think I was also so relieved that we were both alive, that I wanted to be able to cry and cry in private, without being asked if I needed a psychiatrist. It took me a long time to come down to earth.

When I took the little tiny person home, who was lying on a special mattress, all tucked up and asleep at only 10 days old, I still felt a sense of euphoria. I remember seeing her on her little bed, on top of my bigger bed, and thinking that she was an angel who had plopped down from heaven as a present for me. A reward for not giving up on life.

I was also frighteningly aware that the responsibility for giving this person a secure and happy childhood was entirely mine. There were people around to help with some of the practical tasks, but no one was going to share with me the actual responsibility for making it all work. This I felt to be awesome. I was probably more conscious than most mothers of the mistakes it is possible to make as a parent, as I had spent such a lot of time unpicking the tangle of my own childhood. I also had to remember that this child, a little girl, was not me born again, but was a new individual, in another time and another place, with another life to live.

I think that my own early experience has, however,

defined goals for me in my role as a parent. Despite all the work involved, I want her to grow up feeling like a reward rather than a burden. I also want her to grow up feeling that the world, and everything in it, is as much hers as anyone else's, and that she can be a powerful person who can affect her world as she chooses. I also want her to know that she is beautiful, touchable, lovable, and not alone.

Living on a tight rope

Most of the time, of course, I do not think along these idealistic and ambitious lines. My mind is full of far more mundane things, like where the other sock is. From the day we were due to leave the hospital, a huge amount of my time and energy has gone simply into organising the help we need. Asking for help does not come easy. I had been pretty independent as a single person with a couple of hours home help a week, just to do some of the heaviest housework and shopping. With a new-born child, and a painful and temporarily weakened body, the circumstances were completely different. Our situation was not one which it appears was ever expected by any of the statutory services, so there were no 'ready made' support systems to tap into. I have had to create everything for myself, including a rota of friends who would come and sleep-over once a fortnight so that they could take over for a few hours when I was at my most exhausted. I look back on this time with both horror at my vulnerability and neediness, but also with nostalgia for the intense closeness and 'aliveness' I felt with the good friends who responded to the situation by jumping in and sharing the details of that part of my life. Those friendships were deepened for ever for all of us and for Lucy – what a wonderful start to her life!

Until I became a disabled parent, I do not think I realised what an invisible group we are. There are no books, films, TV characters, plays or anything else which portray the life and experiences of being a disabled parent. I can see now how this contributed enormously to my fear that I would never be one, but it has a more insidious and dangerous effect which I am only just beginning to understand. The initiative I have had to have in order to manage my life with Lucy has been a never-ending necessity because, it seems, no one can imagine or work out in advance the fact that we will need assistance to do such and such a thing, or that we might be in a state of urgent need, unless I constantly spell it out. No one offers help, they only respond, and quite often, people do not respond in an appropriate manner until I have painstakingly explained the whole story, including the implications of their saying 'no'. I must say that generally, given all the information, people are extremely reasonable and generous, but the effort required to enlist their support cannot be understood unless it is something you have had to do yourself.

Part of my problem, I am sure, is that I live in London with all its pressures on people to lead frenetic lives. Most of us feel as though our lives are full-up, with no time to give to long-term 'needy' people. I have had to learn the art of spreading the load, widening my group of supporters, returning in some other ways the 'favours', researching and organising paid support, stretching inadequate state benefits, dealing emotionally with the unavailability of certain people, saying goodbye to many temporary helpers, and constantly training new people to take their place. I am sure that doing this, creating these fine balancing tricks, has taught me a great deal, as well as being a welcome education for many non-disabled people who have come into close contact with us. But I do not think I could ever do it again. Seven years on a tightrope, and many more to come. There must be better ways in which communities can work together than this.

'Let's Pretend'

My relationship with Lucy is very intense. I think being a mother and daughter alone, as we are, is a very special kind of situation. Very demanding. Lucy has always been a deeply social person, always wanting to be engaged with someone, talking, playing or sharing an activity with someone else. All my efforts to interest her in sensible, constructive activities such a playing with Lego, or doing puzzles, have failed miserably, especially if she gets a whiff of an idea that this is something she might find herself left to do on her own. Lucy's only real idea of play is to be the script writer, director and leading lady in her own plays, with me or any other person playing all the bit parts. Or I have to animate a dolly who takes over my role in the play. I can only play like this for about ten minutes before I feel an overwhelming need for a cup of tea, or to fall unconscious on the floor. I do not know why I find it so hard, but I do. I can only manage if we have agreed time limits so that we can change the activity to something I find a bit easier, like watching Sesame Street together, or having a bath. At the same time, I am aware that this kind of imaginative play is an absolute necessity for Lucy. I remember once I was cooking dinner and she was trying to get me to be some character or other in a pretend game, and I said, 'No, I'm cooking dinner and I need to concentrate on what I am doing.' She paused for a few moments, and then said 'I know, let's pretend that I'm your little girl and you are my Mummy, cooking dinner.' I thought, 'Is this child crazy or what?' and then realised that what she had done was take control of the situation – she was the director again, not me. This is probably what is behind most of this kind of play where children take over and adults become subordinates. The role-reversal must be a very important way of dealing with feeling so powerless in an 'adultist' world, and must therefore be a good thing. The trouble is that most adults do not understand it, and hate it, and even if you do think you understand it, it is very difficult for us to do because of our need to be in control. However, if adults won't co-operate then children will attempt the same strategies on other children, and then you have a recipe for disaster.

I think I came into parenthood with unrealistically high expectations of myself. Some of this is to do with my background in the theory and practice of Re-evaluation Co-Counselling, a unique source of information about how people think, grow and develop their sense of self in the world. I started out as a mother with personal experience of the healing powers of 'good attention' and was very determined to put that knowledge into practice in my parenting. This in some ways made life easier, especially when Lucy was young. For example I am quite clear that crying is a good thing and not a sign that I am being a terrible caretaker. Once I have checked that all the child's current needs for food, and so on, are met, I can quite happily sit and hold and croon at a screaming baby for a considerable time. Once you realise that you don't have to 'make the baby stop crying' most of the tension goes out of these situations. The issue is only your stamina and eardrums, and possibly lack of sleep.

When Lucy was very little, I was absolutely delighted when she got frustrated with her bricks or whatever, and would crawl all the way over the floor to hit me in order to deal with her anger. I felt like a wonderful, magnaminous resource for her. This has not remained so easy as she has got older, partly because she is bigger and stronger, partly because her verbal skills have developed to such an extraordinary level that it is very difficult not to get caught up in the content of what she is saying to me, and its 'unfairness', and partly because most other people do not understand or share the same perspective on Lucy's behaviour or my response to it. I find, therefore, that I am having to fend off their interference or advice at the same time as being Lucy's counsellor.

In reality I think it is difficult to give to our children those things which we never had ourselves and, whatever age our children are, we are unconsciously being reminded of ourselves at that age. Often we feel a complusion to just repeat whatever behaviour was meted out to us, and sometimes we are objective enough to know that that behaviour was not useful, and discipline ourselves to try something which we hope is more rational. It requires a lot of effort, and our children usually are not even grateful!

For me the effort has paid off though. The child who is now 7, who lives with me, is a delightfully impossible person. Many people do not find her 'easy' but I do not know of anyone who does not like her. It seems to me that she expects adults to be on their best behaviour towards her, and consequently they are. I often see people putting aside their tiredness and distractions to have a good play with her. I remember, for example, a group of sullen-faced reluctant young men on Community Service who had been commandeered by their organiser to lay our lawn for us. They stumped in through our front door and out to the back garden, without looking up from the floor or saying hello. Lucy, aged 2, crawled around the front room to collect her plastic rake and shovel and announced that she was going to help the 'mens'. When I looked out of the window ten minutes later, there was a group of laughing, animated men all sitting around Lucy, meekly taking orders – 'Roll my sleeves up', 'Help me dig this hole', 'Fetch my dolly'. They did eventually lay the lawn as well, for her.

Signing consent forms

My role as a manager of the medical aspects of Lucy's disability has been the most challenging. It is the role I find hardest to write about now, because I still feel myself to be in the middle of it. When I had Lucy, I had to learn about brittle bones. Even though I have brittle bones myself, I knew almost nothing about the condition or the latest thinking on its management, nor had I any inclination to find out. It was completely different when I suddenly had the responsibility for someone else's treatment. I couldn't find out enough. The only really useful source of information was the Brittle Bone Society, not the medical profession who, for the most part, knew even less than I did. I am quite glad of this because it meant in practice that they were all quite relieved to leave all the decision-making, and care, up to me. My own early hospitalisation had taught me very clearly that hurt children need their Mums (or some other really familiar and trusted adult) more than they need anything else, so when Lucy had fractures, I kept her at home and looked after her myself with the support of my friends. I was perfectly confident about it, although I cannot begin to describe what the experience actually felt like at the time. Or what the waiting for 'it' to happen is like, my heart leaping into my mouth at every sudden cry.

I kept this up until Lucy was 4, but then she broke both legs at the same time, and I just knew that this was more than I could handle alone. I took her to hospital and stayed with her for five weeks during which time I helped to put her into traction, which is the nearest equivalent for me of reliving a nightmare. I also decided to sign the consent form for her to have a 'rodding' operation (a metal rod inserted through the length of her femur to act as an internal splint) during that stay, and had to face my terror that she would never wake up from the anaesthetic. I kept rushing into the bathroom to cry and shake during that hospitalisation, reappearing all red and blotchy. I do not know what the many onlookers made of all that emotion, or the situation itself, which must have looked awful to outsiders. But I feel very proud of us both. Lucy does not seem traumatised by the events at all, and I somehow 'came to terms' with the very similar events which had happened to me as a child, but which I had to deal with alone. This time I was in the powerful adult position, and I had more than one willing shoulder to cry on. It was a good job I did, because it was only the first of a series of medical dramas and emergencies which may not yet be over.

The other side of the chasm

When you are expecting your first child, everyone tells you what it will be like, how your life will change, how tired you will be and so on. What no one can prepare you for is the love that makes all other loves pale in comparison. It is not just how your life will change, but how *you* will change. You cannot know that in advance. Once I had become a parent, I felt as though I had crossed to the other side of an enormous chasm, never to return. On the side I had left were all the non-parents I had known and felt so much like. Now I could hardly see them in the mist.

Before I had crossed over this chasm, I had spent many years being a disability activist. As Lucy grew older and we had to emerge from the very private sort of honeymoon world we had inhabited into the wider, public world of nurseries and schools, I had a terrible shock. I had thought that the last ten years of the hard work we in the disability movement had put in, must have made a difference to such a crucial service as education. I had assumed that things must have moved forwards at least at the same pace as they had in other areas, such as employment and independent living. But no. Seeing things from another viewpoint, the other side of the chasm, I became aware that our movement had barely touched the lives of disabled children. The connection between disabled children and the adults they are to become has, amazingly, not been made. For young people, the crudest forms of segregation are still the norm. Even worse, non-disabled educators cling to justifications of such segregation based on the most profound ignorance as to the real issues for, and needs of, disabled people.

I do not believe in enforced segregation of any people from each other. (Self-chosen autonomy is something else.) I think that the only way forward for disabled people is to grow up alongside everyone else, so that this stifling ignorance on the part of non-disabled people can be ended. Our needs are only 'special' in that they are unmet, and this is what 'disables' us. We must make sure that the next generation of architects, doctors, designers, town planners, journalists, teachers, parents not only includes disabled people amongst its ranks, but also recruits non-disabled people who are aware of the full breadth and depth of human experience, so that all future provisions can be inclusive rather than exclusive.

With the knowledge I have, I could not consider sending

Lucy to a segregated school, but the alternatives are not ready for me. Just as I have had to initiate and maintain support systems for myself as a disabled mother, so I am finding that the possibility of a decent mainstream education is something I am having to create almost from scratch. For example, there are currently no proper wheelchair-accessible mainstream schools in the whole of Inner London. We are literally starting at toilet level wherever we go. Because widely held misconceptions about children with disabilities or learning difficulties have never been challenged, there has been little concerted effort to put into practice even the weak existing legislation such as the 1981 Education Act. Where good practices in integration do exist, they can always be traced back to the initiative of one enlightened individual, often with personal experience of disability, who is somewhere high enough up the hierarchy to experiment. A potential revolution is left to personal whim.

My struggle to build a fully supported mainstream placement for Lucy has inexorably led me into a new phase of activism. The challenge is enormous and the stakes are so high that I do not feel that I can lose. As long as I can hang on to the belief that I will eventually win, I feel this to be quite an exciting challenge, a real chance to make the world a little bit better. (In the odd moments when I think we are going to be defeated, I just want to kill!)

Different ways of being

Recently, I have watched a couple of programmes on the television about the terrible 'plight' of marriage, and the 'deplorable' increase in the number of single parents. That is one of the reasons that I am very glad that this book is being published. I feel that being a single mother has been an extension of everything my life as a disabled person has been about – exploring the many different ways of being, the different ways of doing things and of understanding things, using those understandings to create better 'models' of humanity. These debates about fathers being forced to pay, or single mothers not being given council houses, punishing us for not conforming, are about as superficial and banal as it is possible to be. I could write a whole book on my relationships with men, and with Lucy's father in particular or about her relationship with him. Or about his oppression as a disabled person, and a mental health system survivor. I could describe how, between us, we have carved an oasis out of potential chaos. But I won't, because to follow any one of these threads would mean that I would have to challenge and unpick so many assumptions, myths, and traditional forms of thinking, that I would not know where to begin.

I know that for Lucy and me, being a single-parent family works well. My unusual circumstances have opened the door for many people to become closely involved, and I often think we are more like a nineteen-parent family. Everyone concerned feels they have been enriched by the experience, and we have never lost sight of the fact that the main thing about becoming a parent, under any circumstances, is that you get to give life to a new, unique, priceless human being. In a society which really valued young people, parents would not be relegated to the same status as pet-owners, as we currently are, but would be given every assistance necessary to do a good job despite any unfavourable circumstances. Single parents would not be seen as deviants, failures or social problems, but as people to be cherished and supported as life-givers, not resource-takers.

FEELING SPECIAL

JENNY MORRIS

Reciprocated love

My daughter, Rosa, was born 9 years ago, the most important thing ever to happen in my life. Becoming a parent was everything and more than I ever expected. The experience grounded me emotionally, reconciled me to my own childhood and enabled me to love and be loved in a way which healed the scars of my own insecurity and neediness.

I cannot remember ever feeling loved when I was a child. I cannot remember my parents ever touching me with affection. My memories are of anger, of coldness and boredom. My memories are of desperate loneliness, of countless times when I wanted to kill myself. From the age of 16, I searched desperately for warmth, affection and love in a series of sexual relationships with men. Within these relationships I could not stop myself being destructive of love; I had no ability to sustain a comfortable intimacy, for my childhood had given me no opportunity to learn such skills.

Until I was 30, I never thought seriously about having children. If I gave any consideration at all to the matter it was to assume that to have a child would be too restricting of my life. If an acquaintance told me she was pregnant I was quite unable to enter into any form of congratulation, let alone the joyful empathy which I observed in other women. But in 1980, I stopped taking the Pill and a desire to have a child hit me with an irresistible force. My menstural cycle developed into a clear pattern of an overwhelming wish to become pregnant followed by a relief that I hadn't and a fear that I would never be able to cope if ever I did. I remember, during the weeks of desire for a child, working out in exact detail how I would organise my life to make parenthood possible, while the weeks when the desire had gone felt empty and flat.

Then, in the summer of 1981, my mother told me that she had discovered a lump in her breast and that she was going into hospital for a biopsy and possible mastectomy. I told myself that if she had cancer, then I would try to get pregnant immediately rather than wait until I had finished the teacher training course on which I was about to embark. At the time, I justified this decision in terms of a realisation of both my mother's and my own mortality. In retrospect, I recognise that any excuse would have done – I just wanted to have a child.

The relationship that I was in at the time was probably reaching the end of its natural life, but Mick also had a wish to be a parent. We have never lived together and did not intend to now, but told each other that, even if our relationship did not last, we would still have a relationship as parents. I started to track my ovulation cycle and within three months I was pregnant.

I was very conscious throughout my pregnancy that I had no ambivalent feelings whatsoever about this child that I was welcoming into my life. I never panicked, never worried about how I would cope, never doubted that I had the capacity to mother. Which seems very strange, in view of my own emotional immaturity and neediness. Once I was pregnant I felt completely fulfilled and self-sufficient. This, of course, resulted in the ending of my relationship with my daughter's father. I am not proud of the way that I used him, and many of my friends criticised me for not wanting to even see him during my pregnancy. However, I did keep my side of the bargain in that I was always very clear that he did have a role as a father and, from the beginning, I created space in which he could develop his relationship with his daughter.

Just before Rosa was born, I qualified as a teacher and completed the PhD which I had started five years previously. I was living in a beautiful one-bedroom council flat which seemed perfect for a new-born baby. I decided to claim supplementary benefit for the first year as I wanted to stay at home and look after my baby before getting a teaching job. The summer of 1982 was hot and I spent many afternoons, both before and after the birth, walking on Hampstead Heath and eating cream teas in the Hampstead Tea Rooms with a friend whose baby was born six weeks after mine. I organised a rota of women friends to come round and do the housework and shopping for me in the week after Rosa was born. I felt very supported and part of a community. I went to a few, very few, meetings – I had up until then been an active member of the Labour Party and a Labour Councillor – but a lot of that summer and the ensuing year, were spent with other women and their babies and small children. Most of the time, however, I was on my own with my baby. I was never lonely, I never felt isolated or scared, or any of the other things that mothers on their own are supposed to feel. I loved the home making which went with full-time mothering. I got such a pleasure out of turning second-hand clothes (both for me and her) into ours by washing and ironing them. The move into a two-bedroom maisonette – just across the road from my previous flat – was magical in the way that the space gave me the opportunity to create something that was mine and my child's.

The most magical part of that first year was what it meant to become a mother. I had always assumed that I would love this child, completely and utterly, but I was not prepared for the way that she would completely and utterly love me. It had never occurred to me to expect reciprocated love. I remember that a friend, who had two young children herself and who in many ways fulfilled the role that my own mother should have fulfilled for me at that time, made a remark which just astonished me. As I sat there, in her kitchen, comfortable in my unconditional love for my beautiful baby, she said, 'Look at that, mutual adoration.' And I realised that she was right – not only did I love this child, but she loved me back.

Rosa was one of those babies who are immediately in and of this world from the minute she was born. I felt that she came with a ready-made personality and, in spite of the fact that she looked the spitting image of myself as a baby, I never felt that she was me born again. She was, and is, too much her own person. Strong feelings were too dangerous in my childhood for me to feel passionately about things. Rosa's life, in contrast, is full of passion. She is passionate about animals, particularly horses and cats, passionate about her friends. She can express anger and sorrow at the drop of a hat, and the next minute be the sunniest, happiest child imaginable. I feel proud that I have created the space in which she can grow and I feel grateful that she has enabled me to come to terms with my own childhood.

The break

A month after Rosa's first birthday, the day that I signed the contract for the full-time teaching post that I had just been offered, something happened to me which is every new mother's nightmare. While Rosa was fast asleep in her cot, I had an accident which permanently disabled me and took me away from her for five months.

When I had started taking Rosa to her dad's flat each weekend for him to look after her, at first for a few hours and then for a day, I used to be filled with fear that while I was away from her something would happen to me. That evening my fears were realised when I tried to rescue a child who had got stuck on a ledge over the railway line which ran at the bottom of my garden. I fell and broke my back. My legs are permanently paralysed and I now use a wheelchair.

On one level, my emotional self-defences very efficiently looked after me when this happened. While waiting for the ambulance I arranged that a neighbour would contact Mick and get him to come and look after Rosa. I never doubted that he would move into my flat and look after her competently and lovingly. Over the next weeks and months in hospital, I concentrated on getting myself physically into the position so that I could look after her (for example, I did weight-training to learn to lift her on to my lap), getting a transfer to a wheelchair-accessible flat, and initiating legal action for compensation.

On another level, I was terrified and heart-broken. I was terrified that I would no longer be able to live on my own with my daughter; heart-broken at the severance of my relationship with her. During the early days in hospital, I decided that it would be unfair on Rosa for her to grow up in a single-parent household now that I was disabled and Mick and I planned, therefore, to live together. In fact this would have been disastrous but everyone went along with it because we all assumed that a disabled woman would not be able to bring up a child on her own. Luckily, the council could not find us the three-bedroom flat which we insisted on if we were to live together and instead offered me a two-bedroom ground floor property and Mick a one-bedroom flat above it.

By the time I left Stoke Mandeville Hospital, it was clear that I could look after Rosa on my own. It was also clear that the only relationship that Mick and I could have was as parents. He has continued to be a good father to Rosa. She spends twenty-four hours of every weekend with him, alternating Friday and Saturday nights, and one week every summer. He is a permanent and secure fixture in her life and she loves him very much. She has no concept of his being separated from her and her life.

In the first two days after the accident I did not want Mick to bring Rosa to the hospital to see me because I was in such pain and I would not be able to cuddle her in the way that I assumed she would want. However, when he did bring her to see me, the third day after the accident, she didn't seem to want anything to do with me. This remained the case throughout the time I was in hospital, even when I started coming out at weekends. I told myself that such a young baby was only interested in who was looking after her, and Mick had completely taken over my role in that way. If that was the explanation for Rosa's lack of response to me, then she was not suffering as a result of the break in our relationship and I found my own agonies of jealousy and grief easier to deal with than any recognition of the emotional pain that she might be suffering.

It wasn't until a year after I came out of hospital that I was able to think about whether Rosa's lack of response to me might have been the result of feeling abandoned because I had suddenly disappeared and stopped looking after her. Having confronted that possibility and acknowledged the awfulness of that abandonment, however, I am still not sure whether she did actually feel abandoned. She was only 13 months old and it really did feel at the time as if the replacement of one loving adult with another was not a problem for her. In many ways, it was my replacement of Mick when I came out of hospital when Rosa was 18 months old which I think had more of an emotional impact on her.

Getting back

It was very difficult to get back the 'specialness' of my relationship with Rosa after I left hospital. It felt as if the bond with her had been completely severed. Physically, I was looking after her from the moment I moved into the new flat with her, but emotionally it took almost a year before I could truthfully say that it was as if I had never been away. During those five months that I had been in hospital, Rosa had been closer to her father than she was to me, and – in retrospect – that time was a gift both to her and to Mick in that they now enjoy a closer relationship than they might otherwise have had. However, the closeness had been achieved at the expense of the severance of her bond with me and it was heart-breaking to recognise this.

My life was also difficult because I started work full-time four months after returning home. At the time, I was attempting to insist that nothing had changed as a result of my disability, that the structure of my life remained the same. The price of this was exhaustion, and if it had not been for the twenty-four hours each weekend when Mick had Rosa, I would never have survived. I used to sleep for ten hours then and spend the rest of the day catching up on preparation for the next week's teaching. And yet I was also engaged in local disability politics and started to do some research, in addition to my teaching job. I must have been mad.

My memories of those years are pretty blurred. I do remember that, until Rosa was about 4 or 5, I used to get her into bed by seven most nights, then make my supper and collapse in front of the television for the rest of the evening. I watched all sorts of rubbish but it kept me going. I remember feeling guilty that I was so desperate to get Rosa to bed so that I could have time to myself. I would force myself to read her stories every night but most of the time I wasn't enjoying it. If I hadn't been confident that she was having a wonderful time during the day, with her childminder and at the nursery class she went to when she was 3½ years old, I would have been totally consumed with guilt.

The good times during those years were when I was grounded at home with Rosa for long stretches of time. I remember when we were snowed in one year and how wonderful it was not having to worry about time, about rushing to get to work, rushing to get back. I would never have been able to carry on working full-time were it not for college half-terms and holidays, when I could cease looking at the clock every other minute, and instead allow myself the luxury of slowing down and paying attention to Rosa.

Three years after my accident I received £350,000 in compensation. I immediately bought a three-storey Victorian house – just as the house price boom was about to take off – and converted it, installing a lift. Rosa and I now live in this huge house whose spaces we seem to fill quite adequately. A year after that I went part-time in my job and then, finally, last year I felt confident and motivated enough to earn my living as a freelance writer, consultant and researcher.

Gradually, after I started to work part-time and as Rosa got older, I have emerged from that desperate intensity of coping which characterised the years after my accident. There is so little stress in my life now that I cannot conceive of how I managed during those years. Ironically, however, I discovered while I was working very intensely at writing for three months last year, that I was again not paying attention to Rosa. My mind became so consumed with the ideas I was developing that it had little space for her. Maintaining a relationship with my daughter requires a concerted attempt to create emotional space for her, otherwise I become merely a 'good enough' caretaker.

Moving carefully

It both amuses me and fills me with anger that the stereotype of a disabled single parent means that many people will assume that Rosa is a deprived and disadvantaged child. Nothing could be further from the truth, but I am aware that I have to be careful to make sure that this stereotype does not dominate the way that people such as teachers react to my daughter. When it comes to choosing a secondary school for Rosa, for instance, I am uncertain as to whether I will play a full role in looking at schools. Quite apart from the problems of access, which I am not sure that I want to get in the way of deciding on a school, I am aware that strangers make all sorts of negative assumptions about us as a family and I don't want these to influence teachers' expectations of Rosa.

When Rosa first started at primary school, I and another parent, who is also a wheelchair-user, tried to persuade the school to take on the issue of disability in terms both of access for disabled parents and for disabled children. I became Chair of the governing body and helped to ensure that physical access into the ground floor of the school was improved. We started to discuss how the first and second floors could be made accessible and also tried to enthuse the teaching staff and the Parents' and Teachers' Association about the possibilities of the school welcoming children with physical disabilities. We failed in both these goals. Teachers and parents were too frightened of what they saw as the problems of having disabled children in the school and our needs as parents were seen as a special case which could not justify the expenditure. In contrast, the PTA has put enormous effort into raising £20,000 in order to install a play structure which is unsuitable for children with a mobility impairment and thus creates yet another barrier to such children attending the school. Their attitudes provoke such anger and frustration in me that I realised that I had to separate out my feelings about non-disabled people's prejudices against disabled people from my feelings about my daughter's education. On most other measures, the school is a good one and Rosa has always felt very, very positive about going there each day. In order to remain positive myself about the school, I have had to suppress my feelings about its discrimination against disabled parents and children, a discrimination which is found throughout the entire education system.

At the same time, I think it is important that Rosa recognises the prejudice and discrimination which face disabled people, in the same way that it is important that she recognises – and feels able to challenge – racism and sexism. I have to move carefully between my anger that this September she will have to move upstairs and I will no longer be able to visit her classroom; my despair that other children have harassed her because her class has been kept downstairs for two years longer than they would otherwise; Rosa's conflicting feelings about moving upstairs; and my wish that school should remain a positive experience for her.

Most of Rosa's activities outside our home occur in places which are physically inaccessible to me. The drama class which she goes to, the music club, most of her friends' houses – all these are places where I cannot enter. I have developed strategies for dealing with this. Most of her social life takes place at our house. While I was a college lecturer, I was able to organise my timetable so that I could pick Rosa up from nursery and then school at least twice a week. It was easy to start inviting her friends back for tea and now that I work entirely from home I am able to do this most days of the week. I bought a car telephone, so that even if I cannot go into the houses where she goes to parties or to play I can at least make contact and establish that I have brought her or come to pick her up.

Fear

Another legacy of my accident is my fearful realisation that life is very dangerous. I was always a cautious person but now I feel as if disaster is lurking in every daily activity. I can watch Rosa and her friends playing, or getting in and out of the car, or running down a country lane on holiday, and create a vivid picture in my mind of injury and death. I experienced absolute terror when Rosa started going horse riding. When I was first admitted to Stoke Mandeville Spinal Unit there were two girls in the beds opposite me who were both paralysed as the result of riding accidents – one of them had lost the use of both her arms and her legs. How could I possibly let my daughter engage in an activity which could have such devastating consequences? But I do.

Every Saturday Rosa spends half the day at a stables, riding, helping out and just being around the horses. I put up with my terror for her safety because her enjoyment of this activity increases the quality of her life so much. The separation of what riding means to me from what it means to her is part of her growing into an entirely separate person with her own passions and priorities.

Being on my own

People assume things about you if you don't have a sexual relationship. This isn't surprising. We are all so influenced by the idea that we need sex and that if we don't have it then there is something missing, something even wrong with us.

I have assumed for years that my desire for solitude, my need for solitude, is pathological, that it came from what was wrong about my childhood. Undoubtedly it did, but believing that the need for solitude in itself is wrong has prevented me from celebrating this aspect of my self.

More recently I have started to recognise my need for solitude as a part of my self that I value, perhaps above all else. While I've been a parent, I have tended to use Rosa as an excuse for not allowing another adult to become part of my life. I didn't want someone else to enter the life that she and I have, so my relationships have been conducted during the times when Rosa is at her father's. My 'twenty-four hours a week relationships' as one man described them. This has caused difficulties, not least because when someone embarks on a relationship with me my disability makes it into a bigger thing than it may otherwise have been. Casualness has been completely missing from any sexual relationships I have had since being disabled. This is because, in our disablist society, people do not enter lightly into a physical relationship with someone who has a physical disability. How could they? There are so many barriers and inhibitions to be overcome.

The problem has been that the people with whom I have had sexual relationships since my accident thought that the physical disability was the barrier. But once this became neutralised they found that there was something else in the way. Days when I wake up on my own, in an empty house, when the hours stretch ahead with no one else to populate them but myself, these are my life-blood, and when my one day like this a week disappears into a relationship, I start to disintegrate. I can blame it on being a single parent – how necessary it is to have time for myself when my daughter is such an important part of my life the other six days of the week – but, if I'm honest, it was like this even before I had her. With each sexual relationship I've had in my life, after the first few months I would start gasping for solitude. During the later stages of my relationship with Rosa's father I would grab at 'free' weekends; I became the 'I want to be alone' stereotype, all the time feeling guilty, pathological.

It was when I – finally – had a relationship with a woman that she enabled me to confront the fact that a need for solitude is at the central core of my being. And that this need is a positive, not to mention productive, part of me. Above all, it is solitude which has turned me into a writer. Being a mother is not a substitute for a relationship; Rosa will grow up, leave home and lead her own life. It is my autonomy and solitude which are very superior substitutes and I cannot imagine wanting anything more.

The stereotypes which associate happy holidays and cosy Christmases with two-parent families and lots of children meant that I always felt I had to provide Rosa with a surrogate 'family' at Christmas and holiday times. Up until two years ago we would either go to a friend's house for Christmas day or invite other people over to us. But 'family' Christmases have disturbing emotional legacies for me. In my childhood they often ended with my mother retreating to her bedroom in anger and frustration and a cold disappointment settling over the house. So for the last two Christmases, Rosa and I agreed that we would spend Christmas Day on our own but would go over to a friend's house at tea-time. It feels as if our family of two is sufficient at a time when the social pressures telling us that single-parent families are inadequate are particularly strong.

As for holidays, Rosa *is* deprived in that she is the only child in her class who has never been on an aeroplane or a foreign holiday. This was initially because I have no desire to take such a holiday, although I think that I may well have forced myself to by now if it were not that Rosa is so happy with the kind of holidays which we go on. We have settled into a pattern of going to a village in Sussex where a friend has a bungalow. Up until recently I thought that I needed to invite other children to spend time with us there, otherwise, I assumed, Rosa would be bored with only my company. In fact, all that Rosa wants to do when we go there is spend half the day with the woman opposite who has six cats and the rest of the time at the stables down the road. She enjoys having her friends to stay, but this year we are going to be there for most of the weeks entirely on our own. I think I may feel the lack of adult company, although I will find the experience interesting, but once again I feel very liberated from the social pressures which tell me that I cannot provide a proper family for my child.

Feeling special

When Rosa was younger, outings to the theatre, museums and so on, felt very special to me and in fact they still do. Establishing that somewhere was accessible and that she and I could enjoy something which other mothers perhaps take for granted, felt like a real achievement. In the early years after my accident such things took on a magical quality because while I was lying in hospital I could not imagine doing anything so ordinary as taking my daughter to a Saturday morning puppet show. Each time therefore that we did something like this it was an affirmation that life was still wonderful.

The specialness that I felt with the discovery of how I loved being a mother is now mixed up with the specialness that I feel because life has gone on and got better since my accident. I remember spending one Saturday afternoon, when Rosa was 6, going with her on my electric three-wheeler scooter down to the local shops to buy books and paints for her and me, coming back along the canal looking for ducklings, Rosa chatting happily away all the time. Our companionship, her enthusiasm, my ability to buy whatever we wanted, our return to a wonderful house, felt very special. I didn't analyse why at the time, but thinking about it now, such things seem nothing short of miraculous when I consider the legacies of my childhood and the way in which my accident almost brutally destroyed our life together.

JESSIE AND KIM

PIPPA MURRAY

Beginnings

The birth of my first child, Jessie, who is now 10, was the most joyfully overwhelming experience of my life. Immediately she was born I felt a huge, unconditional, mutual love begin to grow between us – something I had never experienced before. When she was born I was not living with her father but we moved into a house together when she was 3 weeks old. The intention had been that we would be moved and settled by the time of the birth but the practicalities of buying a house took longer than expected. Two years later I had another child, a son this time, Kim, who is now 8. By the time he was born I had separated from the children's father and was living happily alone.

Before I had Jessie I had been working full time. When she was born I found I wanted to spend more time with her than a full-time job allowed and luckily I was able to return to work on a part-time basis. This arrangement suited us all well and was just financially possible. After Kim was born, in spite of being a 'single parent' of two very young children and having no extended family nearby to help and support, this was a relatively comfortable time. I had a part-time job, childcare, regular contact with their father, a comfortable flat, just enough money, a social life and plenty of friends willing to babysit. In spite of the hard physical work I felt privileged and happy.

On the day that Kim was born, his father visited and noticed something odd about the shape of his head. I rejected the idea that there might be something wrong with him, as if some instinct was making me push it away. Kim's babyhood was very different from Jessie's. He constantly had small problems. He cried a lot, slept little, had feeding problems, and developed slowly. I suppose somewhere inside I always felt there was something wrong, but it wasn't until he was 1 year old and had his first major seizure that I 'knew' it. I took him to the doctor – and from that moment on I entered a whole new world, the existence of which I had previously had only a very hazy knowledge.

I had to face the fact that Kim had real problems and my life, which I had managed well up until then, both practically and emotionally, seemed to fall apart. For the first time I felt isolated. I felt my friends couldn't help me. They were frightened of what was happening and frightened by Kim. I was frightened, too. My family were too far away to be involved in my life and had their own grief about Kim to deal with. I looked to my children's father for support but we had grown too far apart. I was truly on my own.

Taking action

It has been a pattern in my life that when faced with an emotional problem I ignore it by immersing myself in a practical project. Eventually either the problem would resolve itself or I would gain enough emotional distance to be able to 'forget' about it. This time it was different. There was no apparent resolution, there was no forgetting. My feelings had to be tackled, faced and lived with. I did, however, embark on a practical project at the same time. Eighteen months after Kim had been diagnosed as 'developmentally delayed' and 'epileptic' we moved from London to Sheffield and started work on an intensive home programme to aid Kim's development.

The decision to move cities was obviously a major one. It went hand-in-hand with the decision to give up paid work and to work intensively with Kim. It meant leaving friends and, for the children, moving away from their father. Like all major decisions it was influenced by many things but, really, what lay at the bottom of it was the lack of financial flexibility I had as sole wage-earner with two dependants – one of whom needed more input than he was presently getting at nursery or at home.

When Kim was first diagnosed as 'developmentally delayed' and 'epileptic' the consultant told me not to think of the future. From that moment I could think of nothing else. Would Kim ever be independent? Would he be able to talk? Would he ever be able to work and have a social life? Would he be able to live alone?

At that time, it felt as if the health service professionals were saying that all I could do was to sit back and wait and see how Kim developed. What if I did this and he was not independent? What then? I read as much as I could about children with a developmental delay, anything I could get hold of that made me feel less isolated and taught me about this new world that I had entered, anything that gave me ideas about what might influence how Kim would be as an adult.

After doing a lot of this reading and just living with the situation for a while, I felt there was only one course of action open to me. On the surface, choices existed, but inside myself I felt I had to spend a lot of time working with Kim – not only for Kim, but for Jessie and myself because the more work we put in at an early age the more chance he would have to be independent.

At first I had started working with Kim on a home programme which demanded ten minutes every day of trying to do a chosen task. Before long this did not feel enough and I decided to embark on a six hours a day programme developed by the British Institute for Brain Injured Children. In order to do this programme we needed more space because it required a lot of equipment and room for Kim to be able to do lots of physical activity. After looking at various flats and houses in London it became obvious that I could get nothing bigger there at the same price. The only alternative was to move north and swap the flat for a house.

I felt time was of paramount importance. Jessie was 4 and it made sense to move before, rather than after, she started school. Time was important for Kim also, as everything I had read about disability suggested that the earlier work began, the better the chance of improving the child's quality of life.

So by the time Jessie was 5 and Kim was 3, we were settled in a house in Sheffield attempting to start a new life. A very strange and different life. In order to carry out the programme for Kim I had to find at least fifty volunteers to help every week. This in a city I did not know, where I had few contacts and one friend. So I went to the local press for publicity. I recruited the volunteers but, through the publicity, found myself and my son with labels around our necks. I was a 'single parent' with a 'heartbreak appeal' for my 'brave' son.

It did not take long to find fifty volunteers. The tear-jerking, assumption-laden articles had their use. In spite of the fact that I felt a bit of me was in cold storage, these people took away the sense of isolation I had felt around Kim with my friends in London. Each of the volunteers came to our house because they wanted to work with Kim. They accepted him just as he was, they enjoyed him, they were interested in him and they wanted to do their best for him. The feeling of isolation I had had around him had gone and we soon had many friends and a place in the community. The programme also gave me an adult environment because between nine and five every day there were always three or four adults in the house working together. We had fun doing the programme, because we wanted to make it fun for Kim.

For Jessie, the move to a new life was harder. She had left her father behind in London and she felt, and feels, strongly about him. The house was always full of people doing something for her brother. Looking back I feel I let her down a bit at that time, but then I felt I was doing it all for her as well because it created a possibility that Kim would be more independent when he grew up and she would thus be more free as an adult. I never imagined her physically taking care of him but I knew that she would have a responsibility towards him as his only sibling. At that time, I felt I wanted her to be free from that if possible – both practically and emotionally.

Initially the programme worked incredibly well for Kim. Within a few months he started to babble, as babies babble. Within nine months he came out with his first breakthrough into language, and then couldn't be stopped. From about the age of 3, he had had the odd word, but now, one day at a party in a small house where there were lots of people – the kind of situation he hated – he suddenly said 'Home, home, home, home'. It was the first time he had ever told me what he wanted and he was telling me so clearly. It was wonderful. That just seemed to release something in him and he started talking in four- or five-word sentences. His speech wasn't clear but he could make himself understood. It felt like a wonderful start.

Over the next couple of months he came off anti-convulsive medication; he was brighter; he was developing very quickly; he was beginning to recognise words and numbers; physically he was gaining strength; he was running, walking, riding a tricycle. He had a wonderful time. He enjoyed the programme. He revelled in the intensive attention that he was getting from all these adults. Every volunteer that came into the house gave Kim something different.

And then, after he had been on the programme for about a year and a half and was doing so well, he started to have fits again. This time it felt as if the fits were worse. Medication didn't help much and he just seemed different. He wasn't communicating so well with the outside world. Subtle changes happened which, as the years went by, became huge changes in how he was.

I now know that Kim had caught some kind of viral infection which affected his brain and, although it was not evident at the time, his life had changed drastically for the worse. Four years later, in spite of having tried every drug available and a special diet, in spite of continuing with the programme and then stopping it, he is still having at least one major seizure every day and many minor seizures.

Vulnerability

It has taken me a long time to understand, and therefore to accept, the change in Kim. When he first started having bad fits I regarded it as a temporary upset, as did all the professionals involved. It was simply a matter of finding the right anti-convulsant medication and his seizures would be controlled. Unfortunately Kim seems to be one of the tiny minority for whom this is not true. It has been painful watching him regress and not understanding why. It is painful watching him fit for hour after hour, sometimes day after day, and being unable to comfort him or stop the cause of his discomfort. I grieve that his quality of life is not as it was. His future does not hold any great hope of an improvement in seizures – there is always a chance of improvement but there is also a chance of deterioration and there is the probability that he will go on having regular seizures. This of course affects his chance of gaining independence and, in turn, affects my future. Any ideas I have of what I might do in ten years' time have to be couched around 'providing Kim is able to do this' or 'providing Kim is happy and well cared for'.

I watch Kim persevere with different things. He is so patient and works so hard – if I don't understand what he is saying he will repeat himself as often as I ask or he might try to find a different way of saying it. He rarely gets angry or gives up. Such effort humbles me and I try to take some of his philosophy into my own life. He constantly looks for ways around things and, when he is well enough, enjoys life to the full. If I, with my good health and all my abilities, were not to do the same I would feel I was letting him down very badly indeed.

One thing that Kim has taught me is the value of health –

mine and others – and our huge vulnerability. Any one of us can very easily become brain-injured at any time. All it takes is a fall, a blow on the head, an illness – to mention just a few possibilities. I watch healthy children run, play, speak, laugh, communicate and I marvel at the ease with which they do it. All the things I took for granted before, I now find miraculous.

For several years after I knew Kim was brain-injured I rejected perfection. Watching a ballet, for example, was painful because it excluded him. Now, however, I marvel at that perfection and enjoy it to the full. My sense of enjoyment and appreciation is far greater than it would have been 'before Kim'. And so I find I don't feel comfortable with negative assumptions about what Kim has brought into my life. Although it has taken eight years of hard, emotional work to arrive at where I am today, I feel that Kim has put more joy into my life than I have ever had before.

As the mother of a child with special needs, I feel very vulnerable with regard to the medical profession. For example, I recently read a medical report about Kim, the conclusion of which was that Kim's condition would be better managed if his mother was able to work more closely with professionals. I found that extremely hurtful and felt damaged by it. It is hard to always be strong, to always be sure that what I'm doing is right, so a comment like that can throw me into a crisis of self-doubt and insecurity. I find it incredibly sad that professionals find it so difficult to listen to parents and value the way we want to live.

At the time the report was made the question at issue was whether I have a separation problem with my child. Again, this was a clash of viewpoints. I felt that a particular hospital was not the best place to leave Kim which is what they wanted me to do. It was 200 miles away from where we lived and it wasn't the right environment in which to leave Kim. And this was all turned back on me. I was accused of having a separation problem.

The reaction of one doctor to the worsening of Kim's

condition has been 'Send him to boarding school and have him home at weekends. Then your life won't be so hard.' Again, when I say that this wouldn't solve any problems, I am accused of having a 'separation problem'. If I could find a school I felt was right for him, I would send him, but I won't send him just to make our life easier. It's one of those emotional choices that I can't make.

I find it difficult to accept that Kim is being treated as something other than an 8-year-old child. He is *not* 'an epileptic', he is a child who has epileptic fits. Of *course* I have a 'separation' problem about the idea of my 8-year-old child going away to boarding school – if *Jessie* were suddenly carted off to boarding school both she and I would have significant 'separation' problems. Why should it be any different in the case of Kim? He's like any other child. He breathes, he bleeds when he falls over, he's happy, he's sad. I find it very destructive when the label that is applied to him comes before his humanity.

Jessie

I feel that the negative assumptions behind the stereotyped picture of poor, downtrodden, depressed single parent with the additional 'problem' of a child with a disability have negatively affected some people's view of Jessie. When she first started school, not surprisingly given all the changes in her life, she found it very difficult to settle down. She did not feel comfortable with the teacher and she used to cry in the classroom. Instead of really giving her time to say what she was feeling, it was assumed by the teacher that she was losing out because I was a 'single parent and spending so much time with Kim'. She was being defined through other people's images of our family. It was not until, aged 8, she moved into the Middle school that this weighty label became less distinct. She also became happier and more motivated in her work.

Jessie and I are very close. We are very open with, and sensitive to, each other. I am certain we would not have that depth and quality of relationship if there was another adult in the house. I value that relationship with Jessie. It means that at some levels we are equals and I like that. When I was a child I was brought up as 'one of the children', very different from adults. I don't feel that with Jessie. I really feel she's a very strong little person in her own right, one who is blossoming out. When things are particularly bad with Kim she'll rush around offering to help and fetch me things. If she sees me looking tired she'll give me a hug and say 'Are you all right, Mum? Do you need a cry?' I think if there had been another adult in the house she would have been blocked out, not allowed to take that role, a role she enjoys and one which gives our relationship so much. As in all adult/child relationships there is, of course, an imbalance of power. I am aware of the potential I have to exploit her good nature and to make emotional and practical demands on her. In a sense, Jessie is an only child. She doesn't have a brother that she can play and argue with, be silly with, have good times with.

Parenting on my own

In London, with friends who had known me before I had children, when I was in a relationship, and then later when I was on my own, I never felt anything but me. I never felt I was being labelled in any way. With the move to Sheffield, I almost felt I took on a new identity because of the label which was now attached to me. I was a 'single parent' working at home with a 'brain-injured' child with another young child to look after. I was being defined by my children, by the fact that I had no paid work outside the home, and by the absence of a man.

I do not feel comfortable with the negative assumptions lying behind the single parent label and thus I don't often think of myself as a 'single parent'. I'm a woman, living with two children, parenting them on my own. There is an assumption in the 'single parent' label that life would be easier if I had a male partner. I'm not sure that that is true. There are undoubtedly times when I wish I were sharing my life with another adult. Sometimes I wish there were someone else to do the washing up that's waiting for me downstairs and that everything – whether practical or emotional – was not always up to me. I get so tired at times that I want to curl up into a ball and sleep and sleep and sleep and not look after anyone for two or three weeks. Perhaps if there had been someone with me the last eight or nine years I wouldn't have felt so tired. Perhaps, also, I wouldn't feel so pulled in two a lot of the time. If Kim is poorly when Jessie needs to be taken out somewhere, I have to choose between two conflicting needs. If there was someone else around, then the problem would be solved. If there was someone else around I could occasionally have a lie-in, occasionally sleep through the night.

However, I don't feel that parenting with their father or another male partner is the answer for me. When I had just had Jessie and we were living with her father, I became aware that I was mothering him emotionally. I didn't want to do that, he couldn't see the problem and so we reached an impasse. I feel much happier now I am not mothering another adult. When I look at friends who have a child with a disability and other children too, I am not sure that it is automatically easier if the male partner is around. The woman can still be expected to look after the children and have tea on the table at a certain time. She can still be doing the majority of the domestic chores and mothering an extra person, her husband, as well. I am free of that. I can concentrate on the children and looking after me. I can be very single-minded about our life.

Recently I have gone to several meetings of a group of single parents with children with disabilities. In spite of having enjoyed meeting and talking to other women, I have not felt comfortable in this group because of the assumption that our lives must be hard, lonely and depressing.

I am constantly aware that living on my own with two children greatly enhances the relationship I have with both of the children, but also my relationship with myself has definitely changed as a result of our family set-up. Over the years, through the love and the grief, the good and the bad times, I have had no one to fall back on, to pick up the pieces. At times I have felt very, very distressed and unhappy. However, in order to get over and through these difficult times I have had to look at myself in depth and detail, and come to terms with my whole self. I feel more complete a person for having done that. I am stronger, more centred, my feet are on the ground. I am aware of my limitations. I am more realistic about myself and I know and like myself better. For me the catalyst for this introspective journey was not parenthood on its own, but single parenthood with disability.

Looking back and looking forward

Ten years ago I would never have chosen to give up working in the adult world and it is not the role model I would have chosen for my daughter. But now I feel that maybe what I have done is not such a bad role model. I would rather she grew up as a compassionate and caring person than someone who only valued the world of paid work and maybe went short on the caring. I used to think that I would not want Jessie to be tied down by Kim when she is older and hope that she would get free of the situation. Now, a bit of me hopes that she will have the compassion to be involved, at some level, in her brother's life. I don't have the same set of values that I had ten years ago. I feel that working in the home has made me value relationships and the home world much more, and to question some of the things which I previously thought more important.

My life changed radically as a result of having my children. Within four years of becoming a parent I had changed from full-time work to not doing any paid work. When I first stopped work, moved to Sheffield and started the programme I did not miss going out to work. Organising and running the programme, the ordinary aspects of bringing up two young children and the work required to keep a house going, left me with little time or energy to miss anything from my previous life. I enjoyed the company of all the people who came to help, I enjoyed the atmosphere we created in the house and I enjoyed seeing Kim happy and progressing so well.

Since stopping the programme, and Kim going to school full-time, I have again found myself isolated. I miss adult company. I am beginning to think about going back to work and building up my own, separate life.

Because the main part of my life is invisible to other people I find that I often feel inadequate with other adults. I feel I haven't got interesting things to talk about in great depth because my whole life is consumed by what's going on in our family. At times I feel cut off from the outside world and as if I have nothing to contribute. I feel my relationships with my friends have changed in the last few years. After having Jessie I was able to work, to enjoy a social life. When I first had Kim, although I found it harder, I did the same. As he began to get ill, things changed. When he was first diagnosed I felt a subtle change in my relationships. As the years have gone on and our lives have become more difficult and more different from that of my friends and their children, I have felt an imbalance in most relationships. Many friends, with the best of intentions, come to see us as being 'needy' and so the relationship loses its equality. I am aware that I cannot practically support my friends and their families. I feel sad that I am not close to any of my friends' children when often these friends have close relationships with mine. I miss my old relationships a lot. I am aware I cut off possibilities of friendships by not staying up late or going out a lot – eight years of interrupted sleep takes its toll.

However, if I can find a part-time job and make satisfactory childcare arrangements for Kim in the school holidays, and for when he is not well enough to go to school, I am optimistic that my adult relationships will become more equal and satisfying.

When the children were very young, I was aware of being

different from the many nuclear families around us – both friends and strangers. I would dread Bank Holidays and Sundays. We would go out and all I could see was nuclear families enjoying themselves. I felt our family was incomplete. I was aware that I did not want the children to feel this. Jessie has always been very attached to her father. She thoroughly enjoys the time she spends with him and misses him greatly. I did not want to add to her grief a feeling that we were inadequate as a family – a view reinforced by the media, my family, schools, etc. In time, my feelings of 'incompleteness' went and today I feel that this particular family is very complete indeed. With my increase of strength I have noticed that Jessie no longer yearns for her father. She loves and misses him but feels secure. She has a strong feeling that he is in her family.

However, while Jessie reguarly visits and stays with her father, Kim does not. She is therefore dealing with her feelings of having two parents in separate places on her own. I can never take away the grief I have caused Jessie – I can only try and listen to her when she talks of that grief and give her emotional support through it. How successfully I have done this will be her story when she is older.

As I come to the end of writing this, we are at a time of great change. Jessie and I have been for a week's holiday together, leaving Kim at home with friends. I have applied for a part-time job. Kim is to change school as his present school feels it can no longer meet his needs and he would be better in the special care unit of a school for children with severe learning difficulties. As always, I have a mixture of emotions – relief that changes in Kim are being acknowledged, grief that my son who was once scraping by in a mainstream school is now headed for special care.

I think about the future in a different way from my friends who have children with no disabilities. I cannot take any independence once the children have grown up for granted, as most parents do. It seems extremely unlikely that Kim will ever be completely independent. So, the possibilities of freedom for me when the children are older become less probable because I will have Kim and whatever arrangements I make for him as an adult, he will still be my dependant.

Many people talk about 'coming to terms' with having a child who is chronically ill or disabled. I think that is the wrong way to think about it. I feel that I can *accept* the fact that I have a child with severe problems, but it doesn't make it any easier emotionally, and I don't feel that I can ever, emotionally, come to terms with it. At every stage of Kim's life something new will crop up which highlights how different things are for him than for a child without a disability. There are times when the old grief, which may have been familiar to live with, rears its head again, stages where it becomes freshly traumatic.

Sometimes, when I get into a conversation with a boy child, I will suddenly wonder how old this boy is, and whether he is about Kim's age. Then I'll have real pangs of grief, wondering what Kim would be like if he had not had the brain injuries that he has. It is not that I want him to be different. I love him as he is, but the grief is there and the wondering about what he would have been is there, and it hurts.

Having two children and being so close to both of them feels a very great privilege. My life is immeasurably richer because of them. They have taught and do teach me so much. They have allowed me to change and accept those changes. They have taught me the meaning of total commitment. Whatever mistakes I make in my parenting they forgive me and we can move on. I was not prepared for this aspect of parenting – I knew it would bring love, enjoyment and hard work – I was not aware of the emotional and spiritual growth it has brought.

I've grown to be proud of the way we live together. I'm also proud of the way that I cope and the way I've been able to give myself to these two children. It's the best thing I've ever done in my life, I'm doing it better than anything else I've done and I'm proud of that.

BRINGING UP ELLA

EILEEN PHILLIPS

At the age of 28 I knew I wanted to have a child. I wasn't that convinced that I was able to sustain living with a man. When I discovered I was pregnant, the shock and delight were completely tangled up. I cried my way through the next weeks as I made up my mind that even if I ended up without her father, jobless and homeless, I still wanted the baby. In fact, things did turn out the way of my worst fantasies, but once Ella was born the belief that this was the best thing I was ever likely to do took complete hold.

The point of no return came when I told my parents the news. I remember visiting them in Buckinghamshire, where they lived at the time, and almost leaving without saying. When I finally did tell them, my mother immediately decided we should have a drink. It was never made clear whether this was to steady her nerves after the calamitous announcement of a grandchild whose father was living in the Caribbean, or whether we were all in fact celebrating. Neither she nor my father breathed a word of criticism or the fear that she probably felt as much as I did. Their generosity is something I hope I can emulate when/if Ella ever comes home with something shocking to say.

Friends were more mixed in their responses. Some thought I had no idea of what was in store (I didn't) and that I must be dissuaded before I regretted it (I wouldn't). They feared for a child with an absent black father, living with a white mother in racist England and being rejected by both black and white children. While knowing there was something in what they were saying, I felt hurt. This fed into my growing sense that only I could know if it was right to have this baby and that all I could know was that I wanted it. I have since been asked for advice by women trying to decide whether to go ahead with a pregnancy as a single parent. All I have ever seemed able to say is that you can't know what single parenthood will be like but you *can* know whether you want a baby or not. If you do, you find a way of dealing with the difficult and humiliating problems you may face.

Other friends wondered what the fuss was about, simply accepting I wanted a child. During a pregnancy which I often found unbearable, their pragmatism was reassuring. I watched my body expand, fascinated and horrified. Unable to smoke or drink or stop falling asleep, I felt as if my whole life had been taken over by this greedy being growing inside me. At ante-natal appointments I would stare at happy couples and imagine that having the father by your side made it all a much less frightening and lonely experience. The enormous physical disorientation, coupled with losing my job (a teaching contract not renewed once I had said I was pregnant), and having to find somewhere to live, almost overwhelmed me. And yet it didn't. The strangest thing was the increasing certainty that I was looking forward to the baby as I had never hoped and longed for anything else before.

Her arrival was all and more than I had imagined. It was a new kind of love affair involving twenty-four-hour devotion and I was amazed how unquestioningly I gave it. Unsurprisingly, her father felt threatened when he arrived in this country two months later. His needs and desires got, at best, a perfunctory recognition from me. In so far as they intruded on the care I was giving her, then he could expect growls and snarls. Meanwhile I continued my adoration of this tiny bundle with her complete grip on my heart.

When I fell out with her father and we agreed he should return to Dominica, I faced what I had been half preparing for. And I was both ashamed and proud of my aloneness.

Wheeling her down the street in her buggy I would fiercely return inquisitive or disapproving looks. Inside I would feel hurt, imagining people having bad thoughts about this energetic and delightful baby. How could I be in the wrong, having helped her come into the world? But I would also watch mummies and daddies with their offspring in the park and feel guiltily inadequate. Our family unit did not fit with what everything seemed to be telling me was only right and proper.

I knew I was not enough for Ella, that she had to have more adults in her life. She needed people different from me, allowing her to start constructing her world rather than simply absorbing all that I thought, felt, did. But this knowledge, which meant I welcomed friends and family into caring and responsibility for her, was different from that cold sense of exclusion and vulnerability which regularly hit me when I confronted the fact that we were not a nuclear family.

No doubt I was half-demented from sheer physical exhaustion, but simple little situations would sometimes send me reeling off into high-level anxiety. Such as when the health visitor stopped me near the council estate where I was living and accused me of ignoring Ella's appointment for her measles injection. At the time I was living off social security and fitted well into social services' categories of parents to keep an eye on. Before Ella's birth, I had worked as a lecturer and wasn't used to the state treating me as a deviant. But, instead of responding with all the middle-class outrage I could muster – I had, after all, decided not to keep the appointment because I wasn't keen on immunisations for illnesses which wouldn't leave permanent damage – I shuffled my feet and promised to go next week.

I went, incredible as it sounds, because I was scared they might take Ella away from me. The state terrified me and I wasn't used to feeling that scared. No doubt lengthier exposure to public agencies' attempts at domination teaches some skills at self-defence. But for me, social workers, health workers, were dangerous for the first time. And although this was pretty irrational, it did reflect two quite real things. One was that a large proportion of the population are regularly treated as if they are stupid, incompetent or even wicked. The other was that I had, despite my fine ideas, internalised the belief that being a single parent was just not good enough. One little slip would be sufficient for them to pronounce me an unfit mother.

Another surprise was the discovery that men could be attracted to the ready-made family we comprised and which required no real responsibility on their part for the baby's welfare. I started seeing a man who was fascinated with Ella. I enjoyed his pleasure in her determined efforts to grow and move and felt freed of the need to disguise my own devotion. He was mixed-race too, and when all three of us were together in public I realised the social approval we, as a presumed biological family, received. No longer the abandoned white woman, a suitable object for pity or contempt, I realised again why women can rush quickly out of one broken relationship into another.

But I knew I didn't want a replacement daddy for Ella. Neither had I sorted out what my own needs were. Did I want a sexual relationship which would help me remember the pre-Ella me? Something that could contrast with the serious, committed responsible person who was setting about bringing up a child? Or was I on the search for stability and security – somebody who could lift some of the burden off my shoulders? I remember thinking then, and later, that sex was the only thing I might do which was of no benefit to Ella. Everything else in my life was geared towards her and the wish to make her happy and healthy. The sexual me was the only part of my life which had no direct significance for her.

I couldn't decide if this made sex very important or too dangerous to contemplate. I veered between guilt and a determination to enjoy myself. It was a dynamic that I would play out all through her under-5 years. Sometimes it meant I punished myself hard, believing I deserved men misunderstanding me. Other times I knew I needed to hold on to some image of myself as an adult, with desires and expectations, someone who could dare to get involved in uncontrollable situations. The risks I took for myself had to be distinguishable from the comfort and shelter I was providing for her. Otherwise I would simply sink under the maternal bedclothes and they would eventually smother me.

Guilt

I found Ella as a toddler the hardest to cope with. I was able to feel anger towards her for the first time as our wills clashed. Exhausted by her endless energy, infuriated by her impatience at learning to talk, I retreated from any expectations of my own life. My tiredness and depression sometimes erupted into violence, swiftly followed by agonising guilt. It was a guilt compounded by the knowledge that I had little money, I was a white mother of a black child in a racist society and, above all, I had chosen to have her. I could only blame myself as I got more scared of how this dangerous and difficult world could damage my child. It was I who had thought it possible and had obstinately refused to listen to any warnings.

I remember getting obsessed with news stories about parents beating up their children. Another mother, who shared this gruesome interest, said to me she thought that once you had had a child yourself, wilfully physically damaging it became an unbearable and incomprehensible idea. I couldn't agree. My horror was at the sense that it was so near an experience, just over the edge from the day-in, day-out, devotion which I felt had now robbed me of any identity other than as a mother.

I plotted out a thriller which hinged on a conspiracy to take a single parent's child into care. The reader would spend a major part of the story unsure whether the mother was a batterer or not. 'Accidents', coupled with the mother's diary, would sow the seeds of belief that the social services needed to intervene. I was gripped by the contradiction of immense power that its carer had over a small person's life and the enormous burden pressing down on anyone responsible for the physical and emotional needs of an 18-month-old child. I felt terrifyingly vulnerable as I swerved between a continuing knowledge that I could care for her and the doubt that I was 'fit' because I could imagine hurting her.

Somehow things changed and I have no idea why or even exactly when. As Ella learnt to walk, to understand more, to play with other children, I rediscovered a pride and delight in being part of her growing. I am still never sure, out of the two of us, who gets who to change. I know that when I am anxious or depressed, Ella behaves badly and that her uncooperativeness or high-pitched demandingness winds me up still further. Then things shift and, looking back, I can't tell whether I cheered up, my life improved, or whether her ability to keep asking more of life dispelled the morose and morbid me. Chicken or egg, who knows. Whatever the cause, I felt her pulling me back from my worst fears. It was as if she was saying, through her energetic presence, don't waste time complaining about life, get on and live it.

Not long after this improvement in our lives together we went to visit her father. It was an amazing experience for both of us. She was fêted by him, his family and friends, and luxuriated in the welcome. I fell in love again and began to believe we had a future together. We fought as well, all three of us discovering new kinds of jealousies and confusions. Ella's lively ways astonished her father and he attempted to prevent any petulance she exhibited. I kept trying to explain that she was only a child in a strange country, excited but bewildered by the sudden presence of her father. He would claim that she showed the damage caused by his absence as a discipline in her life, that I let her treat me badly, that she needed him as much as I did. Talk like this drove me into a fury, even while I understood that it was all part of his effort to persuade me that we should be a family under one roof.

Ella was intrigued by a whole new set of grandparents,

aunts, uncles and cousins. I watched with some pride as she made friends, played in the river, ate food she had never seen before, danced at Carnival. When we returned she talked endlessly of what people did and said in Dominica and I felt glad she appeared convinced that it was a country she was part of. I began to hope that my fears for her being brought up by a white family were misplaced. She seemed to have unproblematically absorbed her father's pride in being black, and could accept a difference between her and me without being scared or upset or angry about it.

Just over a year later I faced the final break-up with her father when he came to stay with us in London. Together in this country our different insecurities clashed fatally. I had wanted our relationship to continue for Ella as well as for me but when it came down to it, I knew I had to take any decision about living together for myself. Our romance couldn't survive the harsh realities of London life and I knew I would go under if I tried yet more compromises.

It was a strange time as I felt in one way a great relief. Ever since Ella had been born I had carried a guilt about being alone with her. At the worst moments I had attacked myself with the thought that my selfishness had deprived her of her father. If I were less pig-headed, more easy-going, she would have had both of us. But as she reached 5 years old, I was at some sort of peace. Or at least, in relation to being a single parent, I could accept the facts of my life. I had tried and it wasn't to be. And here was Ella, happy, full of the best kind of energy and absolutely unregrettable.

That's not to say that guilt disappeared. I can remember a friend saying to me one time when Ella was ill, that it's the guilt that's the worst. And I was surprised into recognising that my dreadful feelings about her hot face and quiet, exhausted body included guilt. Somewhere I was harbouring a notion that even if I hadn't directly made her ill, I could certainly have done something to prevent it. Obviously crazy, but the feeling hardly budged, however much I rationalised it.

Guilt could also become acute in relation to sexuality. Just as I had always felt that my sexual life allowed a separation between her and me, so I was equally capable of berating myself for either ignoring her or taking it out on her when things went wrong. A little while ago I made her life a misery as I moped about having to face up to a relationship ending which I couldn't quite let go of. It wasn't fair on her, of course, and I can understand why mothers avoid heartbreak situtions. But Ella at 6 is different from Ella at 2. Although I would prefer to be happy and generous, neither of us can remain stuck in a fiction of me as perfectly responsive and her as endlessly expectant. Somewhere along the line we have had to find a way of living together and accepting each other, good times and bad.

Separating

Mothers often say that their child starting school was a momentous point of separation. I had expected, given that Ella had been at nursery from the age of five months, that the first day of school would be a minor transition. I was amazed to discover myself crying my eyes out on the way to work, shattered by the sense that now she had left me. In the office, I spoke to a woman with a grown-up daughter and she immediately understood. Other women told me that however many children you have, you always feel the same when they start school.

It was so wierd and contradictory. There I had been, keen for her to grow and develop, always encouraging her independence, knowing that I needed more space for myself and then suddenly, bam, totally distraught because she would have her own life now and not be my baby. I wouldn't be there in the playground as she sorted out friends and enemies, I couldn't hold her hand when the teacher asked her to do something she couldn't.

Perhaps school is the first intimation that one day they will leave home and make their own way. It seems very important to know that is the future. Possessive parents are as destructive as sexual partners who won't let you breathe. Having seen Ella through two years of school now, I know that there are dynamics in her life which I cannot expect to construct and shape.

I worried a lot when, at the age of 4, she started insisting on being a boy, wearing a boy's clothes and enjoying the fact that she was continually mistaken for a boy. I thought there was some way she was wanting to replace her father in my life, ensuring that he wouldn't return. Simultaneously she could assert herself as different from me, a black boy child rather than a white female. Maybe she was, but I also think she was grappling with the sexism that says girls are quiet and pretty and play fiddly games in corners. A year ago she changed her mind and went back to being a girl in a stroppy sort of way. She seems to have worked out how to be both tough and sensitive and has found girlfriends who like to make as much noise as she.

In her first year at school she ran around with white, middle-class boys. Now, at 7 years old, she seems to have a mixture of black and white friends, although the strength of gender segregation seems to mean she plays with other girls and argues with the boys. (But then I wonder if my own life is that different!) Mostly these days I feel more anxious about me than her. And this doesn't reflect a creeping indifference. It's more that my hopes for her have become rooted in a knowledge that she will make something of life, rather than life damaging her, doing her over.

Work

Combining work with bringing up a child has pressures whatever your situation. But surprisingly, post-Ella's birth, I found that I was more concise and directed when I was out there earning the rent, than I had been when work and social life slid into each other. Absolutely having to get home to someone improved my concentration. Not finishing on time wasn't a possibility so I developed an acute sense of how long something would take. I began to spot delays and problems well in advance, and, more often than not, find solutions which, if not perfect, were at least quick.

I first went back to work on a job share when Ella was 5 months old and I couldn't believe how much I crammed into my four hours a day in the office. I was, of course, nervous about proving my employability and over-compensated dramatically. But once I had calmed down I still wanted to make sure I didn't waste time. I kept discovering that intensifying the rhythm of work made sense. I could make sure I was there no longer than I had to be because I was sifting out what was productive and learning to ignore irrelevancies. And as soon as I went two floors down to collect her from the workplace nursery, the working me disappeared and I was engrossed again in this unpredictable and mesmerising baby.

Of course, the fact that I was able to get reasonably paid work meant that it was financially viable to go to work and pay for childcare. I did do a calculation when I was half-time that I was £5 a week better off having a job than living off the state. But I knew that staying at home would both drive me round the bend and lessen the chances of getting jobs I wanted to do when I felt more prepared to go back full-time. So I stuck it out until my job-share partner left and I accepted the full job.

However, this meant working full-time far sooner than I had intended. I remember it was hell. I was dominated by work simultaneously with anxiety about Ella's well-being. For three months I ran everywhere and never finished a conversation. Then, as with most things, I adapted. The schizophrenia of my life settled into a routine which only occasionally I thought was perverse.

The times I found most odd were being with couples with a baby around Ella's age, the father working and full of the momentous decisions he took five or six days a week, while the mother looked after the baby. Part of me would feel the same old determination I had first had in my teens that being a boy didn't make you 'importanter' than being a girl. I would discuss work vivaciously with the man as if nothing had changed for me. Then I would imagine the woman wondering what the hell I was talking about and how could I undermine her side of the argument as she tried to force him to take an interest in the baby and in her life.

Well, whose side was I on? I didn't want to deny maternity and all its consequences, but neither could I bear the idea that the web of concern and love you feel for your child relegates you to a sphere of domestic irrelevancy. I also knew that the world of work interested me, that there was something which could turn into a nightmare of claustrophobia if all my attention was centred on a child.

The contradictions have lessened as I continued to work and Ella has grown older. Not gone away, but at least not throwing me into the painful self-doubt which used to be always lurking. Giving children the absolute, no questions asked, security of your concern is the best thing you can do and they can get. For a single parent, that part can be more straightforward than when you're caught in the tensions of a relationship with the father and mediating between him and the child. But there is a danger for both you and the child of the concern becoming control. As you give relentlessly to a small person who is materially and emotionally dependent on you, you can begin to assume you are moulding her/him into a certain image, that she/he can act as a replacement for your own repressed or ignored aspirations. The best protection against this is to keep wanting for yourself, then maybe you can let the child breathe too.

I've always been impressed by those women who seem to deal with having children and yet still manage to be autonomous women – sexually active, getting on with life, definitely not 'Mumsy' (to repeat Michael Caine in *Alfie* making his nastiest attack on the girlfriend he made pregnant). The most powerful image of maternity is self-sacrifice and, as an image which forms our own unconscious selves, it is completely incompatible with independence and autonomy.

As a working parent, there are never enough hours to the

day and this is something which can threaten to crush single parents as they try to do battle with numerous responsibilities. But in a strange way this has made me much clearer about the jobs I do. I have very little tolerance for doing work that doesn't either interest me or appear to serve some useful purpose. I now know I can earn my living and I am determined not to put up with doing this on any terms. My expectations are often too high, but generally I prefer it that way and it's something that I think Ella's presence in my life has helped make happen.

I have noticed recently that for the first time I am able to make friends with other single parents. In the past I have shied away from an identification which I presumed was one of victim – us abandoned or lonely or inadequate parents. I never saw myself as a victim although I have felt lonely and inadequate. Somehow the optimism that I feel about Ella has freed me both from resentment towards well-endowed nuclear families and from the wariness with which I've treated other women on their own with kids. I can finally accept diversity, not out of an ideological inclination but because it is part of the life we are living. During the hardest times I thought I could never want another child again. Everything in the world just made it too impossible that I could repeat that crazy, hopeful endeavour. These times are by no means soft and yet I catch myself thinking, well, someday, I can almost believe I could.

BECOMING AN ADULT

DIANA RICHARDS

I was 16 years old and had just left school when I got pregnant, which wasn't too good. I was living at my mother's house and was doing a three-month college course (Gateway to English). When I finished that, the company with which I had been doing work experience offered me a full-time job and I did that until I was six months pregnant.

When I told my mother that I was pregnant the first thing she asked was whether I was going to get married, but I hadn't even considered that. I was too young, I didn't know what I was doing and my boyfriend, John, didn't want to get married either. We were both 16. I thought that I didn't want to have a child because it was going to mess up my life, but by the time I admitted to myself that I was pregnant, I was twelve weeks gone and I felt it was too late to terminate it. It took so long to admit to myself that I was pregnant because I thought my father would kill me. My mother already seemed to know; she kept telling me to stop wearing tight clothes because I wasn't doing myself any good. And I thought, what does she mean? I put on weight really quickly and it showed in my face. I thought I was being really clever, because I was hiding it, but my mother knew all along.

It was easier once my parents knew, in that I didn't have to wear my jeans and pretend that nothing was going on. However, my father's reaction to my pregnancy made me feel so bad. My mother told me to tell him but I was too frightened to, so she did it for me. He stopped speaking to me and that was really, really hard for me. I get on so much better with my father than my mother and he has always meant such a lot to me. Silly things would happen, like my mother would put his food on a tray and tell me to take it in and he would tell me to put it on the table and then he would come and pick it up. It was as if he didn't want to take anything from me or have anything to do with me. That really, really hurt me. He was so upset about my becoming pregnant because he has this idea that his children are his princes and princesses and that we can do no wrong. So it really hurt him when it happened. Among the family that he came from in St Lucia, it's just not the done thing for your daughter to get pregnant at the age of 16. He wanted his children to go to college, to university, to become someone. So as far as he was concerned it was an embarrassment because I was so young and it was a reflection on him. It meant that he couldn't control his kids. Of course he wasn't to blame – I just thought I knew it all and it was my responsibility that I got pregnant. Now I have a child of my own, I can understand how he felt, but when I was 16 you couldn't have told me.

At one time I was thinking of just having the baby and sending it to my godmother in Canada, because she can't have kids. But then one of my aunts, who is only a few years older than me, was also pregnant. She encouraged me, telling me that things would be better once I had the baby. If it hadn't been for her, I think I wouldn't have my son now. The support my grandmother gave me was also very important. She treated me as an adult and gave me all the advice I needed about nappies and feeding and so on.

By the time I was six months pregnant, things were really bad at my house because of my father. So I moved to Birmingham to live with my grandparents and I stayed up there until I had my son. When Michael was born, my mother came up to Birmingham but my father didn't come with her. As far as the outside world was concerned, I was too young to have this baby, but I felt wonderful. He was my responsibility and I loved him as I had never loved anyone else.

I took Michael to London when he was 2 weeks old because I wanted to show him to my father. I needed his approval. I wanted to say to him, this is my gorgeous son, this is your grandson. When I got to my parents' house, my brothers were fighting to be the first ones to hold Michael and then my mum took him and said to my father, 'Look at your grandson.' He just went, 'Hmm,' and turned his head away. She said again, 'This is your grandson,' and she gave Michael to him. But still my father wouldn't talk to me and I went back up the next day to Birmingham. Then, when Michael was 8 weeks old, I telephoned my parents. My father answered the phone, and I told him I wanted to come home. I was crying. He just said, 'You had better speak to your mother'. Three days later my father arrived at my grandmother's house to pick me up and take Michael and me back to London. I was so happy – as I saw him coming towards the house I shouted, 'My dad's here, my dad's here.' It was so important to me that my dad had come for me.

John had been around, off and on, during my pregnancy. He had come up to Birmingham when I thought I had gone into labour but it had been a false alarm and by the time Michael was actually born he had gone back to London. We finally split up when Michael was 3 months old. John was seeing somebody else but I wasn't really bothered because I thought I could cope by myself. The only financial help he ever gave me was that he bought a steriliser and a woolly hat for Michael; in fact he used to borrow money off me until I stopped seeing him. John said that Michael wasn't his son – even though Michael is the spitting image of him. We didn't talk for three-and-a-half years and I only spoke to him then because I thought I had to get his permission to take Michael out of the country when I was going to America. He refused his permission but then I found that I didn't need it anyway.

I lived with my parents for the first two-and-a-half years of Michael's life. Then, during the local elections, we had all these councillors down saying, 'What can we do for you?' I told them I wanted a flat of my own and within six weeks I got a two-bedroom flat in Thamesmead. I was doing temporary office work then because it gave me the flexibility. Michael started going to nursery. I was still spending a lot of time at my Mum's house and we would go there most nights to eat.

When Michael was 4 years old, we went to my aunt's wedding in St Lucia and stayed there for four months. When I came back I did temping again, doing word processing. My mother had just come back from America and she said her sister's brother-in-law was getting married, in New York, and she needed someone to represent the family. She told me to go, while she looked after Michael for me. I really liked New York. It's rough and it's dirty and awful things go on there but I loved it. When I got back I was really restless and I didn't know what to do. Michael was just about to start school.

By this time John was back in touch with us and he saw Michael occasionally, although he was very unreliable. He accused me of being a bad mother because I had gone away to America and he threatened to take me to court. I was getting very down. I thought, I've given up five years of my life for my son; I can't do this any longer. I wanted to go back to America and make a new life for myself. My father said it was better that I went if that's what I really wanted to do. So within six weeks of returning from New York, I was back in America and Michael went to live with his grandparents. I did a correspondence course in hotel management when I was over there and stayed with my aunt until I got my own apartment. I did a lot of babysitting to earn money and I studied during the day.

To get my father's approval I used to send my results home. I would get distinctions and would write and say 'Look how well I'm doing.' Michael was really well looked after. My parents kept all the routine that I had established, like what time he went to bed. My brothers paid him a lot of attention and bought presents for him because he was the only nephew. Christmas time was hard for me because I missed being with him for two Christmases. New Year's Eve was really bad. In my family, you have to be there at midnight on New Year's Eve and as they counted down to midnight in New York, and I watched it on television, I thought I can't bear this.

My 'phone bill was enormous because I would telephone Michael every week. It was amazing when he started to read – I would say 'Read to me, read to me,' when I 'phoned him. I would try to ring him a quarter of an hour before he went to bed so that I could tell him to go to bed and say goodnight to him. My family told me not to telephone so much and not to send him so many gifts. I just felt so guilty. I joined two or three children's book clubs in New York and I would get the books sent direct to London. It got to the stage where Michael would expect something from me every week.

When my family brought him out to see me, I told them not to bring any clothes for Michael to wear while he was there because I had bought lots and lots of clothes for him. I got to the stage where I realised I was not spending any money on myself and I had to stop buying things for Michael out of guilt. People learnt to stop asking me how my son was because it just made me feel so awful. I stopped going to picnics and thing where other people would bring their children.

I still feel guilty because although I missed Michael, I didn't miss him enough to make me go home.

The second year that I was in New York, Michael came over with my sister and I found that he was closer to my sister than he was to me. When he hurt himself he would run to her and not me. I felt I should be grateful to my sister because she had been looking after my child, but instead I felt resentful. I thought she was taking him away from me and I decided I had to come back to London or I would lose my child altogether.

When I did come back I felt that Michael wasn't my child any more and for the first year it was very hard. I was living with my parents and, although my sister was living elsewhere, she still spent a lot of time looking after Michael, especially when I was working evenings. I went back to doing temping and also got a job at a sports centre. I worked very hard so that I could give Michael a good standard of living and I am still doing temping because it pays better than a permanent job.

I want Michael to realise that *I* am his mother, not my sister nor my mother. I want him to realise that he has his own father and that his grandfather is not his father. I want him to have so much, and to do everything that I didn't do. Yet it's rough because I am dealing with it by myself. I feel that to some extent my family spoilt Michael while I was away in America and that now I have to be stricter with him. My father used to be fairly strict with us as children and I want to parent Michael in that way. But there seems to be this gap between Michael and me in the same way that there was a gap between myself and my mother.

I lived with my parents for over two years after I came back from America and then, just recently, I got another council flat. It isn't very close to my parents and I prefer this. All the time I was living with my parents I felt that my mother was telling me that things were better when I was away. My parents treated me like a teenage daughter, complaining about things like making a mess, not doing the washing up and so on. But I am also the mother of a child. I am not Michael's big sister. However, if I wanted to go out I had to ask my mother to babysit so I was still dependent on her. I was still like a little kid, asking permission to go out.

A neighbour said to me once, 'I see your sister is still playing mother to your child.' That hurt. Especially as my mother's comment was that my sister was a better mother to Michael than I am.

I think it was a mistake going back to live with my parents when Michael was just a baby. Once I did that, and particularly once I went back to work, my mother started to take over. My sister was 15 at the time and when she left school she looked after Michael, which was very convenient because it enabled me to go out to work. However, my mother started to say things about my sister being the one who really looked after Michael so she should have more of a say than I did in what he wore, what he ate, when he went to bed.

There were times in America when I forgot that I was my mother's daughter or that I was Michael's mother and that felt good. Perhaps I went to America to get away from the pressures within my family. I am the eldest but my parents think that I've let them down and that my sister has made more of her life. My father is always saying, 'Why can't you be like your sister?' She's got a good job now and her own flat and a car.

I do want to develop a career but I feel that I can't until Michael is older. I wouldn't have other children because that would tie me down for too long. I'm 27 now and Michael is 10 so I'll only be in my 30s when he is 16 and there will still be plenty of time to study and get qualified. Whereas if I had another child now, I would be tied down for another sixteen years.

My mother tries to be affectionate towards me these days. I think she feels that there is a gap between us – in contrast to the close relationship that there is between her and my sister. She makes a point of trying to kiss me and she says that if I let her kiss me then it must be going to rain (which is Black people's equivalent to saying once in a blue moon). I suppose I feel resentful that she never tried being closer to me before, so why is she starting to do that now?

I felt unsurped by my brothers and sister when I was a child – my brother was born after me and my parents were so pleased he was a boy. Then my sister was so like my father and my little brother was so cute. And me, I wasn't like other girls and it seems there wasn't anything special about me. I didn't play with dolls, I would rather play with trains or read a book. I felt left out as a child. My brothers and sister all came one after another, taking my place, and I felt my mother didn't have time for me because she was so busy. I was closer to my aunt and my grandmother, particularly from the age of about 9, when I started spending a lot of holidays with my grandmother. And, in a way, history is repeating itself because Michael spends so much time with his grandmother and aunt.

POLITICAL OR PATHOLOGICAL?

CAROLE STURDY

How do I write about the experience of single parenthood without giving the whole of my life story? To what extent is how I feel and think now determined by that one fact rather than by any number of others, all interacting? These are the first questions that make writing on this topic so difficult for me, because what it's like being a single parent is so much tied up with what it's like being me. They're very hard to disentangle.

In 1967, at the age of 20, I finished university in Canada (where my parents were living) and returned to England on my own. After four years away I had lost touch with my old school friends and for a while was quite lonely. I lived in hostels and bedsitters and took a succession of different, unskilled jobs. My rationalisation for this was that I was looking for 'experience' so that I could one day become a writer. In fact I was feeling quite shaky and vulnerable. I didn't want a stressful job and found manual work, catering jobs in particular, quite comforting.

Partly because of my personal situation and partly because of my political beliefs and the ideology of the times, I saw myself increasingly as something of an outsider. I joined the anti-Vietnam war movement and began to identify myself with those who were loosely termed the 'libertarian left'. It was their slogan that the personal was political which drew me into politics, because it offered an explanation for my own lack of 'fit', and provided me with a ready-made community.

By the time I met Ciaran's father, Rik, it was the early seventies and we were both members of the Claimants and Unemployed Workers' Union. I had also been involved in a couple of women's groups by that time. We didn't fall madly in love with each other. Strong passions weren't a feature of our relationship, at least not until the very end when I experienced very strong feelings indeed. I was drawn towards him at first because I found him very attractive and I very much needed someone at the time, having recently emerged from a long-standing triangular relationship and left behind a whole circle of friends in another city. I now think he was also quite vulnerable and for similar reasons, although I didn't see it then. We had rooms in the same squat in a house in North London. His, I remember, had a large poster of Lenin on the door. He was not long out of university and was quite an accomplished musician although playing music was seen as a diversion, by most of us, from our main activity which was politics.

Our relationship was pretty up and down from the start. I was very unsure of him, perhaps because of the lack of strong feelings, and my low self-esteem. It was also a time when monogamy and the nuclear family were seen by the circles of people we both moved in as reactionary and repressive institutions. There was a naïve belief amongst us that feelings, including those of jealousy, could be changed at will through a process of political discussion. For example, I remember being in a sexual politics discussion group with a woman Rik was having an affair with, early on in our relationship and trying to deal with our feelings about each other, and about him, by discussing, at great length, Engels' writings on the family.

At that time, I and all the people I knew lived collectively in various well-organised squats in North London. There were hardly any children amongst us in those early days. We often debated the question of whether it was a good idea actually to live with the person with whom you had a sexual relationship. Most concluded that it was not, since the introduction of a couple into the sort of collective households we all lived in was always disruptive. To be in a 'couple' at all was something of a taboo. The Red Collective, the political group to which Rik and I belonged, had a view, the details of which I now forget, which held that sex shouldn't be imprisoned within domesticity and that these two types of relationship were best kept separate. These political ideas gave a rationale to something that my fear of dependency, as I now see it, might have led me to anyway: namely, a decision not to live with Rik, ever, not even after Ciaran was born. What I also see in that decision now is an extreme and conventional desire to do the 'correct' thing, as defined by the social group of which I was a member.

I got pregnant when I was 29 and when Rik and I were on the brink of splitting up. Restless to break free from the left-wing moralism we had both subscribed to, he had started playing music seriously again and was beginning to dabble in other relationships. We were not trying to have a baby and I was still using contraception, which was, however, less than 100 per cent effective because I became pregnant 'by accident'. With hindsight, and even then, I suspected that this was in fact no accident. I remember that I had at the time a surge of desire for a baby and used to dream about it constantly. What my motives were I can only guess at now. They were not clear to me then, although I remember trying to think them through. I may have wanted to hang on to my relationship to Rik, if only by proxy. And my motivation may have had something to do with wanting to feel myself a real woman rather than the little girl I still perceived myself to be. Or perhaps I conceived Ciaran with the unconscious desire that through him I could vicariously enjoy all the love and affection that I craved. Whatever the conscious or unconscious motives, my alibi at the time was that Ciaran's conception was a mistake and simply the result of not putting my cap in properly on the night in question. However, the fact that Rik and I did not both make a conscious decision to have a child has inhibited me ever since in arguments with him over maintenance.

Contradictions

Rik was, at first, ambivalent about the prospect of a child but agreed to give me emotional support during the pregnancy and after the birth. He came to National Childbirth Trust classes with me and was not present at Ciaran's birth in hospital. It was an unexpectedly fulfilling experience for me, with very little pain or medical intervention. Rik was supportive and obviously felt moved by witnessing the birth of his first child. When we left hospital, he helped Ciaran and me back home to a warm welcome from the rest of the collective household. They had decked the house with flowers and prepared a special home-coming feast. After that Rik visited every day. Right from the beginning, from his own genuine desire and supported by the ideology of childcare we both adhered to, he took on at least 50 per cent of Ciaran's care.

When, after only five weeks at home, I returned to my part-time job as a nursing auxiliary in the local hospital, Rik's contribution as a father became even more necessary. We got into a rhythm of pushing Ciaran in his pram back and forth between our two houses. I would bicycle off to work and, four hours later, cycle anxiously back again longing to see Ciaran, my breasts aching to feed him.

I can hardly remember now what on earth my feelings were at this time and how long I imagined that these arrangements could continue. Was I satisfied with them? I must have thought they would carry on indefinitely. The situation was certainly good for me in many ways. I was getting a great deal of support from the others in my household as well as from Rik, and I felt part of a real community. But this set-up, supportive as it was in many ways, was not destined to last for very long since it bore within itself the seeds of its own destruction, namely the potential nuclear family represented by Rik, Ciaran and me.

The first hint of what was to come occurred soon after I returned from hospital with Ciaran. It became clear that I wanted a lot of time to myself with the baby. I was prepared to share him to a certain extent but basically I felt that he was my baby, and that I wanted, and had, a special relationship with him. I did not share his care with the others in the house as, I think, they expected. Instead I became very involved in my new, surprisingly intense, relationship. I would put Ciaran to sleep quietly in his cot in my room where I would often retreat to be with him. I became more and more engrossed in this new relationship and began, unconsciously I think, to shut out all others, apart from Rik. Rik became a daily visitor to the house where he too would tend to disappear into the room containing Ciaran and myself. Some of the other people in the house began, understandably, to resent this unasked-for change in the household's customs and to feel resentful. After about nine months of this situation, I was told that Rik's frequent visits to the house were unwanted and were to be discouraged. I felt put in a position where I had to choose between the support offered by the collective and that offered by Rik. It was a hurtful and difficult choice but, in the end, the bond with Rik was stronger so I chose him and decided reluctantly that I had to move out – although not of course to live with Rik.

It wasn't easy to find somewhere else to live because, without a group of other people, it was difficult to set up another squat. I had no savings and very little income so that buying a flat was out of the question. Looking back now it is astonishing to realise how emotionally passive I was being at the time. I did not make any demands on Rik, nor did I negotiate or argue with the other members of the household who had presented me with this choice. I simply accepted it. I can remember feeling scared and 'cast out' on my own, but it did not occur to me to oppose other people's interpretation of the situation. Although emotionally passive, I must have been fairly resourceful, however, because I managed to find another single mother amongst our circle of friends who was also in search of somewhere to live. We didn't know each other but we were ready to team up temporarily and together persuaded a local housing co-operative to let us have a small house on a 'short-life' basis – that is, a house which was awaiting major works to be done. In return we promised that, when work was ready to start on the house, we would move out and expect no further support from them.

Independence and dependence

I had given up my job in the hospital when Ciaran was six months old, so by now I was at home looking after him full time. I was quite poor, but it seemed easier to live on less in those days. Rik contributed very little to Ciaran's maintenance and I did not ask for more. It was very much part of feminist thinking at the time that, to reduce the constraint of women's dependence on men, the state should be expected to support our childcare needs in total. Although politically I felt quite assertive about the state's duty to support women in caring for children, it is ironic that on a personal level I did not feel entitled to make any demands on the individual man I was, supposedly, intimate with.

I was also, by now, becoming more isolated because I had less support at home. I did not enjoy much rapport with the woman I shared the house with. We didn't actively dislike each other, but we had little in common and tended to pursue our separate lives on the separate floors of our small terraced house. I became, therefore, more emotionally dependent on Rik without, however, acknowledging it. In fact, I actively and defensively denied any such dependence. Because I did not have much confidence that I was intrinsically lovable, it was best to prepare myself for the inevitable, which was that sooner or later I would be left alone again.

When Ciaran was about 18 months old, I found him a place in a council-funded day nursery and myself a place on a state-funded training course in shorthand and typing so that I could be equipped to support myself and him in a moderately paid job. I had no great ambitions. Although I had a degree, I felt relatively de-skilled after ten years of doing manual jobs and unable to do anything more stressful or demanding. And while I was commuting into the City to do my course on acquiring office skills, Rik was breaking new ground enjoying some success with the rock group he was playing with. They were playing pub gigs and benefits and had built up quite a following. There was even hopeful talk of recording deals and a US tour. He would often come round to take Ciaran out with the woman who was the drummer in the band. Prone to jealousy as I was, I was naturally suspicious of this lively, attractive woman with pink hair who was always effusively friendly towards me. When I voiced these suspicions to Rik I was quickly assured that she was already living with a man with whom she had a very stable relationship and that she and Rik were, of course, simply good friends. She continued to visit, chatting easily with me whenever she did so, while I castigated myself for my paranoia. My sense of betrayal was all the greater, therefore, when I learned from a friend, what Rik himself later confirmed, that they had been having an affair for some time.

The ending of my relationship with Rik was spread over about six months. It was a terrible time and yet also, I think, cathartic and hence, in a way, deeply satisfying to me. It was almost as if, in some peculiar way, all my unconscious defences had contrived to produce a situation which would allow me the expression of a great stream of repressed feelings of betrayal and abandonment. This was the converse side of the emotional passivity apparent in other areas of my life which often left me feeling perplexed and indecisive. It was with some relief and gratification (almost) that I found myself having definite and strong feelings at last. These alternated between acute sorrow and rage. When overcome by sorrow, I felt myself to be a complete victim, rejected and my trust betrayed. In this masochistic mood, in which my personal qualities, or the lack of them, were to blame for whatever had happened to me, the world presented itself in a frightening and threatening aspect. On the other hand, when rage was the predominant feeling, Rik was a villain whose actions were deceitful, dishonest and cruel. It was as though I could at last express, without inhibition, feelings which were so powerful that they must have had at least part of their origin elsewhere. At these times I became a relentless interrogator of Rik, a counsel for the prosecution, as though I could, by sheer force of logic and argument, change his feelings and behaviour.

In retrospect, I can see that this was probably a painful time for Rik as well as me, but I think it was more damaging to my self-esteem than his because I could not help seeing his leaving as a judgement upon me. I saw myself in the most negative terms as unattractive, asexual, neurotic and uninteresting. It took almost two years for me to begin to feel almost all right again and by that time I was half-way through my first, nine-month-long bout of psychotherapy.

Because closeness in relationships had carried a threat of being 'taken over' by the other person, I had always been afraid of intimacy. Paradoxically, I was most able to express my feelings toward Rik at the moment when our relationship was ending. In a sense, this was the safest form of intimacy that I could conceive. I had a sense that I was re-enacting some other scene of betrayal and at last discharging feelings that had never been allowed expression before. At an unconscious level therefore, perhaps you could say that I chose single parenthood as a creative attempt to solve the problem of my dual fear of being taken over by a stronger personality or abandoned completely. I suppose I had too weak a sense of who I was and of my own boundaries to be confident that I could cope with maintaining my separateness as part of a couple.

This doesn't mean that living alone with a small child was necessarily easy either, so it was not an altogether successful 'solution' to the problem. In fact there were times when it felt unbearable, because I felt like an abandoned baby myself and so found it difficult to cope with the insistent, and competing, demands of my own 2-year-old. This was especially true when I had made enormous efforts to be an angelic mother. Bedtimes were particularly dangerous. When I had bathed Ciaran, put him to bed, read him stories, and cuddled him, I would feel an almost uncontrollable rage when he would not respond reasonably by going to sleep. I couldn't bear to feel so powerless and sometimes came close to hitting him. What I really wanted, of course, was someone to comfort and look after me.

Long-standing conflicts

When I found myself on my own with Ciaran, the 1980s were about to begin, bringing with them the new age of 'hard' individualism and the break up of many collectivist projects. I was also embarking, perhaps not entirely coincidentally, on an individualist phase in my own life, and, looking back, it is extraordinary to remember how quickly, in the space of a year or two, the collective way of life that Rik and I had been part of seemed to evaporate. This new individualist project of being a single parent was also a way for me of resolving a long-standing conflict which, put crudely, had been between being 'hard-headed', using my brain, and giving more importance to the world of feelings and interpersonal relations. Being a single parent was a way of being, of *having* to be both, since I had to support Ciaran and care for him. It gave me permission to have ambition, to strive for success, without sacrificing, through my role as a mother, the world of domesticity and feelings. Being a single parent was a way of *having* to have it both ways in a sense that may not necessarily have been the case if I had been a mother in a conventional nuclear family.

After I split up with Rik, I continued to assume that I had no right to expect any financial support from him. It had been a shock for me to discover how emotionally dependent I had been on him, so I must have worked hard to ensure that I should not be dependent on him in any other way. Not asking him for anything was also, of course, a way of excluding him and was also therefore something of an aggressive act against him, pushing him away. He used to give me small amounts of money when he could afford to, and nothing when he could not. Of course I used to have some bitter thoughts about his definition of 'affordability'. As for me, I have now worked without a break since Ciaran was 18 months old, starting with part-time jobs at twenty-eight hours a week and working up to full-time. I do feel that my responsibility as the only bread-winner in the family is a burden sometimes and does limit my choices. I feel I have to maintain a certain level of income simply to ensure that Ciaran is not disadvantaged.

I now have what I would have labelled in my youth as a 'straight' job working within the NHS. It seems a far cry from the idealistic aspirations of my 20s and 30s. I find my present work quite stressful and long to have a breathing space sometimes, to go back for a while to the way I lived then when I could drift between a succession of undemanding jobs while my main energies were put into friendships, political activity or studying. I would like to have the space to stop and think, and to find some work that could be truly fulfilling and enjoyable. And perhaps I will be able to achieve some of this when Ciaran grows up. For the present though there is at least some gratification in being able to provide a fairly comfortable life for myself and Ciaran.

A few years ago, after I had been in therapy for some time, I started to feel more able to ask for financial support from Rik, and I took out an affiliation order against him through the local magistrates court. In the end the arrangement we came to was amicable enough and we mutually agreed on a regular maintenance payment. Despite this, I have never succeeded in really feeling entitled to financial support from Rik and would, I think, only properly do so if we had both consciously and deliberately agreed to have Ciaran together as our child. I wonder how many children, though, are conceived in such a rational manner? This uncertainty of my right to support meant that when Rik recently left his job and told me there would be no more monthly payments, it was at least six months before I did anything about it. In the end, when the arrears had mounted up to over £600, not knowing what else to do, I simply informed the magistrates court so that they could recover the arrears. He was arrested and marched down to the local police station. He was, of course, extremely indignant about this, and lost no time in telling me so.

Being alone

I am not in a sexual relationship with anyone now and haven't been, apart from a couple of weekend 'flings', for at least seven years. It wasn't always like that. After I split up with Rik I had three consecutive relationships, each lasting several months. They were very important to me and helped me begin to feel all right about myself. But there was a definite point when I withdrew from relationships with men. It certainly became harder to keep a social life of any sort going after Rik and his family (by now he was married with a daughter) moved to North Devon and Ciaran could no longer spend time each week with his father. It was hard to find babysitters and I couldn't afford to pay for them very often. I started to stay in more but not simply for this material reason.

I think that I had caught some glimpses of the complications within my relationship with Ciaran that could be caused by a lover, and they had made me afraid. There was one occasion, for instance, when Ciaran was quite ill. He was in hospital for observation with a condition called an 'irritable hip', the effect of which was that one of his legs would not support him at all and he could not move. The treatment consisted of putting him on complete bed rest for a week or more with his leg in traction. He was about 8 or 9 years old at the time and in quite a lot of pain. I stayed with him in the hospital for the first couple of nights and I remember that, apart from being distressed by his pain and fear, I was also anxious that the doctors were not telling me the truth and that he had something more chronically wrong with him. After the first day or two Ciaran bore it all very well, including the daily blood testing and the uncomfortable nights. He made friends with the nurses, and enjoyed having his own personal TV set and getting lots of visitors and cards. I moved back home after the first two nights and visited him every day.

Every evening when I left the hospital I told Ciaran that I would be there again the next morning at breakfast time, and every morning I was late, sometimes not getting there until nearly midday. I suffered enormous guilt over this but couldn't change my behaviour despite it. I explained it to myself in terms of my extreme neediness at the time, which led me to spend all the time I was not at the hospital with the man I was in a relationship with. It was this that made me less than perfect in keeping my promises to Ciaran and so frightened me of my own neediness that I withdrew, unconsciously, from further involvement with men. Quite simply I did not trust myself.

There was also something else which led me to this withdrawal. This was the tendency of another man with whom I had a relationship to assume the role of Ciaran's father, reprimanding him and even threatening to smack him once without consulting me. Although I cannot remember the details of this clearly now, I do remember Ciaran's distress and indignation, his insistence that Rik was his only real father, and my own failure to intervene. My subsequent guilt and fear of repeating the event was another reason for my withdrawal from relationships, or more specifically, from the consequences of what appeared to be my own all-consuming needs. It gave me a glimpse of the awful possibilities of the scenario that I saw in some child abuse cases; of the needy single mother and equally needy, but violent, stepfather. I found I wasn't so very far from all that myself.

For the past seven or eight years I have, more or less consciously, given absolute priority to being present for Ciaran, and creating a nurturing environment for him. I have memories of many winter evenings spent cooped up in cosy domesticity with him playing board and card games – *Cluedo, Sorry, Snap* – on the living-room floor. The worry I then had was that I was using Ciaran *himself* to meet my needs, and living vicariously through him. I worried that this would be bad for him. When he was about 10 or so I became convinced that the reason he was not doing as well as I expected at school was because he was emotionally dominated by me and therefore didn't have enough space, or experience enough frustration, to motivate his own creativity and thought. This occurred when I was in the middle of my second stint of psychotherapy and tended to interpret everything in psychodynamic terms. My therapist supported the idea of my seeking some help for Ciaran, and this of course clinched it.

I referred myself and him to Child Guidance, much to the surprise of the school who said he was fine, and also to Ciaran's bewilderment, who didn't understand what it was about and hated going. Our visits had no effect on his schoolwork but they did reveal that he became upset at the idea of any man attempting to 'replace' his dad. They helped me by reassuring me that there was nothing wrong with Ciaran, although I was characterised, I think kindly, by the counsellor, as a 'worrier'.

Mothering a son

I have moments of really painful regret for the fact that Ciaran hasn't got a father who is around more often and who is more of a real presence in his life. There is a lot of sadness in the feeling that nothing I do can ever make that up to him. It is simply an accomplished fact that nothing can undo. He sometimes speaks in a wistfully envious way of boys who talk about things that they've done with their dads at the weekend. And when we watch TV programmes about families he sometimes says that he wishes he had a dad like that. I feel sorry that he should experience such a sense of loss and regret, simply because of the way that Rik and I were unable to deal with certain issues in our lives, or took irresponsible decisions when we were younger.

I also think Ciaran feels that it would be nice to have a dad who could physically protect him. I am not very brave in standing up to bullies and I don't think I provide him with a very good model of physical courage. I have often felt inadequate in helping him deal with playground bullying at school. I haven't known whether to advise him to avoid bullies or to square up to them. I can't help feeling that boys are expected to be physically courageous in a way that girls are not and that a father who had been through the same things himself would have been able to help him more than me in dealing with those expectations.

A friend who is a psychotherapist once told me that I treated Ciaran as a substitute husband. That frightened me. Her remark at once raised the dual stereotypes of the emotionally crippled 'mummy's boy' on the one hand, and the dominating all-devouring mother on the other. There must be risks for all children, especially only children, in having a single parent. The relationship is bound to have a particular intensity with no other parent to deflect it. Boys must have to struggle harder to find their identity as men, and the struggle may be given up if there is, in fantasy, the softer option of meeting mother's every need instead. Now that Ciaran has reached puberty I know I must encourage him, gently, to be more autonomous without, however, appearing to reject him. It is difficult because I know I am needy and he is a good companion most of the time. He can be funny, lively and easy to talk to. Thankfully, though, he is also sometimes rude, rebellious and impossibly moody, so my job may not be too difficult. The best way I can help him, of course, is by trying to seek more satisfaction and pleasure in my own life, apart from him. At the same time, I do not want to be so frightened by the stereotypes that I overreact and stop doing things together with him. I still enjoy going to the theatre or cinema with him occasionally and don't want to stop that.

When I first had Ciaran I saw my decision to become a single mother as a political act, in opposition to the conventional nuclear family and the role of 'housewife'. Nowadays I tend to see it as having as much to do with my psychological make-up as with any wider politics. My language of explanation has changed over the years from the political, collectivist language of fourteen years ago to the more psychoanalytic, individualised language that I have used more lately. This reflects, I think, a development in a certain section of the women's movement of my generation for whom consciousness raising wasn't, in the end, enough, and who then went on to explore psychoanalytic concepts for explanations of human behaviour, within, of course, a feminist perspective. Both types of explanation had their drawbacks for me.

Seeing everything from a political, even a feminist, viewpoint didn't always help me to assert myself in my personal relationship with Rik, as I think I have shown. It encouraged an over-emphasis on rationality and the belief that the 'correct arguments' (if only one could work them out) would necessarily prevail. It was very hard for my younger self, when using that sort of language, first, to articulate what I quite irrationally and 'incorrectly' desired and, second, to get it. On the other hand, the language that I have used more recently, pervaded with psychoanalytic terms, sometimes perhaps imperfectly understood, has resulted in a tendency to view every event or decision in my life as yet another example of personal pathology or an opportunity for self-blame. The fact that I am a single parent has seemed to me a particular inadequacy, demonstrating a fear of intimacy and an inability to sustain close and long-term relationships. Psychoanalytic language in the way that I have understood it can be quite disabling in its tendency to be both normative ('every psychologically healthy person ought to be in a couple') and judgmental ('just about everything that happens to you is the consequence of your own unconscious greed, hatred or envy'). I have found such language not only deeply depressing (I accept that some depression is inevitable as self-knowledge increases) but also ultimately unhelpful since it leaves me feeling hopeless.

What I am struggling toward now is a more compassionate

and benign understanding of how I came to be a single parent, and why my situation is as it is now. I can be more hopeful, and self-forgiving, if I work from an assumption that becoming a single parent, like many other events that seemed to just 'happen' to me, came about as a result of my often unconscious attempts to arrive at creative solutions to problems of which I was not even fully aware. More than that, I need to work from a position of faith that such 'creative' solutions are prompted by desires which aim for the affirmation of life rather than towards its opposite.

Writing this article has helped me to see, and, I hope, be on guard against, the dangers of viewing my life as a single parent in either purely political or pathological terms. Both points of view are, in the end, over-simplistic and reductionist and unhelpful on their own. I notice that what I am left with is a language that contains words like 'faith' and 'hope' simply because they must be there for me to understand my experience in a way that is enabling. Is it a coincidence that my changing perceptions of being a single parent, and the language that I use, have followed the trends of the times? After political and pathological, what next?

THE BEST THING I EVER DID

MAUREEN SULLIVAN

I have six children. My eldest daughter, Moira, is 21. Then there is Michael, 20, and Fergal, 18. Bridget is 12, Eileen is 8 and Maeve, the youngest, is 6. We lived in a small village in Ireland until I came over to England two years ago with my two boys. We had a lot of financial problems at home. My husband wasn't working and hasn't been working for years. It was very difficult, we never had anything and we were usually broke on a Monday. We were getting about £100 a week at that time, and that was for eight of us. We used to survive on getting tick at the shop and it was getting worse and worse. We argued.

The boys wanted to leave because there was no work for them there. So I decided to come over to England with them to help them set up. I told my husband I was coming back but I had no intention of doing so. It was quite the best thing I ever did.

I had been over in London for about two years when I was younger, before I was married. And I had loved it. I still had a friend here and I asked whether I could stay with her. So myself and the two boys came over and we all got jobs through an agency. Within a couple of months, I got a friend to bring Maeve over. We're not on the telephone at home so I just got messages to my husband that it would be better to bring Maeve over here because the facilities were better. The kids knew I wasn't coming back and he eventually realised this himself. The other kids didn't want to stay either; there was nothing for them there, no work, nothing.

I knew I was doing the right thing. I needed the freedom for myself.

When Maeve came over I took her to a paediatrician who said that she had Rhett's Syndrome. That upset me a lot because the doctors in Ireland had said she wasn't a typical Rhett's Syndrome Child. I had first taken her to my GP in Ireland when she was about a year and 3 months because she had started not being able to hold things and then she convulsed. He said not to worry but then he referred me to another doctor. Eventually I got sent to see a doctor in Dublin who said that he didn't think she was a typical Rhett's Syndrome child but that she would be slow and she would need to go to a special school. So when the doctor here just said she was Rhett's Syndrome it was very upsetting. What happens with Rhett's Syndrome is that a child loses all his/her skills. Maeve now has no muscles that she can use. She has tablets for her convulsions and tablets to stop her hyperventilating.

I went to the council once Maeve came over and we got housed, but it was only a three-bedroom flat and no garden. Two more of the children came over. By this stage my husband knew I wasn't coming back. Once I had all the children (except the oldest girl) over here, I asked the council for another flat. It took about a year to get this house I'm now in. The GP wrote a letter about Maeve and I got passed on to the housing officer who deals with housing for disabled people. At first I didn't really want to move. I had got to know the area, the shops and things and the people around there. The flats where we lived were mostly occupied by older people so it was very quiet.

When I first came down to see the house where I'm now living, I was looking all around and I couldn't see which house it could be. All the houses looked like they were private, not like council houses. I was so surprised when I saw it. I didn't think it would be as big as this. I didn't think a council place could be like this. It's a house that stands on its own and it's huge. There's a bedroom and bathroom on the ground floor for Maeve, but at the moment one of the older kids uses that because I want Maeve to sleep upstairs at night as she's too young to be left downstairs on her own.

There's a bungalow just next to this house, where Sue lives with her 5-year-old son who has cerebral palsy. She's now my best friend and we get a lot of support from each other.

Eileen, who is 8, misses her dad more than the others. He came over for her Communion this year, although he didn't stay with us. The two young ones went over to see him in the summer and they didn't want to come back here. But they did, and now they're settled here. We're much better off in London. There's no arguing between me and him like there used to be, which couldn't have been good for the kids. It wasn't that he was violent, at least not often, but we were always arguing over money and so on. I'm so much better off financially because I've got the money in my pocket. At home I didn't even used to have the money to give the kids to get into the swimming-pool, but now I have control over the money. And the older kids that are working, they give me money. Moira complains about that sometimes but I tell her that she would have to pay a lot more if she lived away from home.

There are a lot more facilities here for Maeve than there would have been back in Ireland. She goes to a special school each day and is picked up by the bus and taken there and back. They are very good with her there; they do lots of exercises and stimulate her. The social worker told me they're setting up a scheme where Maeve could go to a family for a day once a week to give me a break. They call it respite fostering.

I went with Maeve to Lourdes last year. Bridget and Eileen go to a school which takes disabled children to Lourdes each year. The parish church raises the money and they made so much money last year that they could take four children instead of two. So they asked if Maeve and I would like to go and they gave us spending money as well. Of course you go expecting a little miracle when you come back. And we haven't had one yet. But it did make me feel better. It's just totally different when you're there. It's a whole different world. You can forget the outside world altogether. We were there for a week. You go down to the grotto first thing every morning and there was a Mass every day in a different place. Maeve had Holy Communion there. Every afternoon there were processions. But it's not just praying all the time. They took us on a day trip out into the country. On two or three days they took the children to look after them so that the parents could go and do things. It was like a holiday and a rest. You don't think about the problems that you've left at home.

The week after we came back from Lourdes we moved in here. Moving away from Ireland was the biggest and the best move I ever made, but moving into this house was a big thing as well. It's such a big house, I'm still trying to furnish it.

I have felt very down recently. A few weeks ago I had to go into hospital for a small operation. I was kept in overnight which meant that I didn't see Maeve from the time she went to bed on Tuesday until she came back from school on Thursday. While I was away she was very good but apparently she got very excited whenever my name was mentioned. On the Friday after I came back she started getting fits. Up until then her fits had been well controlled by the drugs she was on and in fact she had been needing fewer drugs. She fitted all day Saturday and Sunday and I kept her home from school on Monday. She woke up several times during each night and each time she fitted. I telephoned my paediatrician who told me to increase her tablets, which I did. After five or six days, she started to come back to normal again and within another few days she was back to her usual dosage.

I was so worried that she had got all these attacks because she missed me and that stress brought the fits on. The paediatrician didn't agree with me but when I took Maeve down to the hospital where she goes for her breathing, the doctor there said that she probably did get like that because I was away. So where do I go from there? Does that mean that

I can't even go on holiday without her? How am I going to get a break, because I think I really need one very soon? At the moment I really feel terrible. I haven't been sleeping and my head feels like a brick fell on it – it's so heavy and I'm just in fits of crying at different times. I just don't seem to have the energy to do anything. I know I'll have to pull myself out of it somehow, but for a few days I just wished I could get up and go away from Maeve and the other kids. But how can I do that if Maeve is going to get fits every time I'm away from her?

Every bit of the responsibility for Maeve is on me. I never get a break from it. The older children are of an age that they have their own friends, their own interests. I think sometimes that the other kids should do more with Maeve but they've got their own lives. They don't like taking her out and this makes me feel that they don't care about her. It is upsetting. I've tried talking to them. I think they don't like taking her out because people stare at Maeve.

The holidays are the worst, when she doesn't go to school and I have her all the time. I don't feel I do enough with her. I feel I should do exercises with her but I get very lazy in the holidays. Sometimes I lie in bed very late. And then we go out to the shops and to the park. She loves doing that. I take her swimming sometimes but I really need another adult with me so that I can get a bit of a swim.

Even when Maeve is at school I don't get out and do things. I want to go and play tennis, to go swimming, play badminton. Sue and I keep saying that we'll go but something always comes up and we don't. She'll say that she can't go because her house is a tip and she needs to clean it. Or I'll say I feel so terrible I can't go out. We don't seem to be able to get the energy to go and do things. But if I stay at home, I just think aboout Maeve and I get depressed.

I've been taking her to a spiritual healer. He's very good. He says that she'll walk and talk. She has started saying Fergal's name. She understands when you talk to her and she loves people talking to her. She loves the kids reading to her and showing her picture books.

I don't think about the future, when Maeve gets older. I just think that the healer is right, that she will get better and better.

A WOMAN ON HER OWN

JEAN WALK

Breaking free

Fourteen years ago, at the age of 28, I fell pregnant with my second child. At the time, my first child, Emma, was 3½ years old. During my second pregancy I finally realised that the relationship with the children's father was wrong. He wasn't the sort of guy I wanted. I had half realised it before and tried to get out of the relationship but I wasn't a very strong person at the time. I needed to be with him.

Gerry and I were never married. For five years we lived together on and off, mostly at his mother's. During the last eighteen months of our relationship we were given a place to live by the council and it was around about then that things really started to go wrong. However, when I fell pregnant with Sarah, he said we should try to make it work. His mother had said he should marry me, and he was willing to give it a go. But the day I had the baby I knew it was over. The feelings weren't there any more; he walked into that delivery room and I didn't feel love for him any more.

What had happened was that I had changed and he hadn't. I was starting to become the person that I had always wanted to be since I was a teenager. What I wanted out of life and out of a relationship, was a partner. I wanted to be friends, to have a man as a companion. I didn't want to be just a woman that's there to bring children into the world, to cook meals to put on the table when the man comes home from work, to sit indoors while he goes out.

For the first four years that I had been with him I think I

had been blinded by what people call love. Sexually it was very good. As a bachelor he's a terrific guy but as a partner he just wasn't there. He wasn't a nasty person or anything like that. He just used to come in, eat, and then go out to the pub. I thought there must be more to life than this. His mum once said to me when I spoke out in company, 'Why don't you just sit back and keep quiet?' I looked at her and thought, this is what my life is going to be like. She would cook dinner for all these men – her husband's mates – who used to come back to her house. And all their wives were just sitting inside their own houses, waiting for their husbands to come home.

It was a wonderful feeling to have that second baby and I felt stronger. I thought, one day I'll get out of this. It took six months before I got him to leave but it took seven years to get him out of my system. Although I wanted out of the relationship, it was hard to get myself back. I had lost friends because I had dropped out of what I had been doing. I had two young children and I had lost a lot of confidence. Although I felt strong in knowing that I wanted the relationship to finish I didn't feel strong on my own. During the first two years I would have taken him back at the drop of a hat. He used to come round when it suited him. To see the kids he said. But the sexual feeling was there and sometimes he would stay the night. It took a long time before I started to feel stronger on my own.

I finally accepted that he wasn't going to come back when he got married seven years later. I didn't really want him back but it was the company I wanted. On bad days, bad nights, I would cry and cry, and want him there. But then I would wake up the next morning and think, 'Oh God, I'm so glad he's not here.' And then, sometimes, when he was there the next morning it would be no good. He just couldn't communicate, he had no way of talking about feelings.

The day that he got married, I went out of London for the day, but the girls went to the wedding. When she came back, Emma told me she had felt like saying something when the vicar said, 'Do you know of any cause or just impediment?

etc' I told her that she knew I didn't want him, but she said that she felt he'd made me so sad.

Surviving alone

When Emma was a baby I had worked as a home help and she went to a nursery. However, I gave up working when I was pregnant with Sarah because I was so ill during the pregnancy. I got Sarah into the nursery when she was 6 months old but spent a lot of time there because I didn't like leaving her. So they gave me a cleaning job – because I was doing it anyway – and then a job as a cook. I stayed there over a year but Sarah wouldn't settle. During that time, I used to see this woman in the park with all these children – she was a childminder – and I thought, 'that's what I want to do.' So I got registered as a childminder and I haven't looked back.

Through the week I felt great, but come the weekend everyone disappeared into their families. At the weekend, I couldn't see the childminders that I spent the week with because that's when their husbands were around and a single woman like me didn't belong in those family situations.

I started to get involved in committees, like the Martin Luther King Adventure Playground. I started thinking that there was more to life than just the kids and I began to go out more socially. The childminders used to go out together as a group socially but again it was only during the week. Weekends were still difficult and I would get down then.

After a while, I started doing fostering. The first child I took had been abandoned and I thought that could so easily have been me. I could have given Emma up. In fact, my parents had offered to take her for the first five years. I could even have been into drugs or drink. After I had Emma, I'd meet some friends for lunch, and we'd have a few drinks and I would forget all my problems, everything was lovely. So I could have easily taken to drink. Then one day I realised Emma was more important and I couldn't allow that to happen to me because I had to look after her.

The mother of the first child I took abandoned her baby

because she didn't know how to love him. She kept him clean and fed him but she didn't know how to love him so, of course, he cried all day. She left him in the park. I heard about it through the Under 5s worker at the Social Services office, a woman called Jill Boon who has been so important in giving me encouragement over the years. I offered to have the child but she said, 'Are you sure? He screams all the time.' When I met the mother and talked to her, I realised there were things that she just didn't know about being a parent. I thought I can do some good here. I feel I found myself then. I knew what I wanted out of life.

As far as men are concerned I want a partner. I want someone who can come in and talk about what's gone on that day. I want someone who enjoys going out and doing things together. Who enjoys talking. But I don't want a full-time relationship now. I talk to the girls about it and they say they don't want me to have a relationship. They want us to stay just as we are. I would like someone to go out with two or three nights a week but I don't want to live with anyone. I don't feel as lonely now as I did when I was first on my own with the girls. I've got more friends and I've got a caravan which I share with a group of people. Even weekends aren't such a problem now.

A woman on her own

Almost all the women I know are married and when we go out together I find that their husbands think that I'm encouraging the women to go out without them. There was one incident when I went out with a friend and she went on to a nightclub after I went home. She got in very late that night and the following morning her husband came banging at my door saying that I was to blame. He went to hit me. His fist came up, I just backed away and he thought better of it.

Another time, on the way home I walked past the flat of the woman that I had gone out with, and her husband collared me as I passed the front door. He wanted to know where she was. She had actually gone off with another man but I said she was on her way home in a taxi. He shouted at me, 'Just because you haven't got a man to come home to.' He was implying that I was trying to take his wife away and encourage her to go out with other men.

When I went out with the other childminders and their husbands, or when we went on holiday together, the men would often make jokes about my being on my own. When we were camping, they would say things like 'We're going to come into your tent and make love to you.' I used to laugh and treat it as a joke but sometimes I would feel threatened.

I've been called a lesbian, a dyke. One woman came round to my house after she had had a row with her husband and a few hours later he telephoned, trying to find her. He got quite abusive saying he knew she was there and that I was nothing but a dyke. I said, 'Well, perhaps your wife's happier with me.' He's never said that again. Other women friends have told me that their husbands say that I'm a lesbian. It's not that *I* think that it's an insult, but *they* do.

Men have funny ideas about women on their own. When Gerry first left, some of his friends used to come round. They obviously thought that a woman on her own with two young children was desperate for a man to go to bed with. In the end I told Gerry that about four of his friends had been round, expecting something, and he warned them off. I had the same kind of trouble with one of the workmen who was doing work on my flat.

I don't think I should hide the fact that I'm a woman on my own but men have all these ideas once they find out.

Some people say that I'm anti-men but I'm not. It's just that I wouldn't tolerate the things that a lot of the women I know put up with. Their whole lives revolve around showing consideration for men; the housework has to be done, the cooking, the kids looked after, all to suit the men's convenience. My life revolves around doing what I want to do when I want to do it. My sister once said to me that the reason I haven't got a man is because I wouldn't clean his shoes or put his dinner on the table. I laughed at her at the time and told her that I had tried it her way but that I hadn't been happy with being the dogsbody. She said that I could not have loved Gerry or I wouldn't have felt like that. She died two years ago. She was only 43 years old and I often wonder whether she was really happy with her life. I know there were things she wanted to do for herself such as learning to drive and going off on her own. She always put her family first, like most women. My other two sisters have started to come down to London to see me for long weekends about once a year. We go off to the theatre and for a meal, without their husbands and children. They really look forward to it without feeling guilty.

How did I get like this?

Ever since I was a teenager I've felt that I wanted more from life than being married to a man who never talked to me. It's difficult to know why I started to feel different from my sisters.

My parents had a fairly good relationship, although my father had money problems. My mother worked to keep the house and six children. She worked at all sorts of jobs, being a barmaid, in a factory, many different kinds of jobs. My dad used to come in from work and just fall asleep. When I tried talking to my mum about it, she said 'That's just part of life.' I told her it was not going to be part of *my* life. I was so different from my sisters that I used to ask my mum if I was adopted. For example, from the age of 14, I used to dress differently whereas my mum and sisters all used to dress the same. When I was 15, I became friends with this girl who was considered by other people to be quite outrageous for Newcastle. She wore the kind of clothes they were wearing down in London. She liked different kinds of music – Bob Dylan and things like that. She was intelligent whereas I never did well at school. We had a terrific time together. I became a hippy and my mum and dad accepted it in the end. In 1968, when I was 17, they allowed me to go to London. I was following a bloke who played in a group although we weren't involved and in fact I don't think he even knew I existed.

I got a job as a chambermaid at the Strand Palace Hotel. My friend came as well and after five months we got our first bedsit. Then I worked in a betting shop, which I didn't like because I wasn't very good at taking bets over the phone as my spelling was so poor. I left there and went to work at C & A and did very well. They were going to make me up to a supervisior, even though I was only 18. However, I couldn't take the strain and I had a breakdown. I suffer from psoriasis and had had a breakdown when I was younger. I had been to a psychiatrist when I was 16 and he had said that if things got on top of me I had to stop. So I gave up the job and hitched around Europe with some friends for five months.

The 60s were an amazing time to grow up. The Vietnam War touched me so much and I'm still very aware of all the awful things that are happening in the world. I can't understand people who don't know what's going on – like with the Gulf War and the Kurds – and who aren't affected by it. I may watch *Corontation Street* but I'm still aware of what's going on in the world.

My two daughters

People think Emma is confident, but she isn't. She's got my insecurities and I get upset about that. Sarah's had a very stable life because right from the beginning of her life it was just me and the girls. But Emma has had a different experience. When I was pregnant with her I knew the relationship with Gerry wasn't going to work and I used to sit there and cry and talk to this baby inside me. So right from the beginning she's been carrying all my insecurities. And I feel bad about that.

Emma feels that we're not a proper family without her dad, although now she wouldn't want him living with us. Now that he's married, the two girls get more out of seeing him because his wife buys them presents and organises meals.

When I've asked Emma why she doesn't think we're a proper family she goes back to the time when he was around. But she was so young I don't see how she can remember that. She says she loved him so much. He was a charmer and he did adore her. They're like two peas in a pod to look at. Whereas Sarah's never had her father around, so she's quite happy the way we are.

Emma bears the brunt of my monthly depressions. I get angry with her and I take it out on her when I'm down. I actually went for help once. I went to a Well Woman Clinic and they suggested I went to a parent's group. But when I told Emma about it, she said, 'Why do you want to do that, we're all right aren't we? You don't need to do that.' She says, 'Why do you worry, Mum?' She says that a lot of her friends can't talk to their mums but she can and we have a good relationship in that way. So then I think perhaps we're not too bad. When Emma was born, I did love her but I didn't feel that bond in the way that I did when Sarah was born. I only realised with Sarah what women meant when they talked about feeling that bond with their child.

Emma and I have been going through a bad time recently. She's 18 and doing an NNEB course so she doesn't have much money. She's always asking me for money and I do give her what I can afford but I get so wound up about it sometimes. Eva, a childminder who lives across the road, says that once Emma's out working it will get easier. I find it very difficult and feel bad that I get so angry.

Where do I go from here?

I've tried to get out of childminding but I'm not qualified to do anything else and I'm not very confident. I work with social workers and I think I would enjoy doing their job. I can, and I do, help the parents whose children I foster, but I'm frightened of anything to do with paperwork. I like working with children and old people. Jill Boon has been an inspiration to me, and she's made me confident. I have been able to go along to meetings, to case conferences and all that.

I can see it from two sides, from the parents' side as well. Who's to say who is a good parent? Who's to say I've been a good mother?

I like doing short-term fostering. I love all the kids I have, but I like to see them move on, hopefully back to their families. I meet so many people through doing short-term fostering. When you've got one child for years and years, that's it, social workers stop coming. But with this, I get involved. It makes me feel important and I find it really stimulating. Like this week, every night there's something going on. There's a meeting tonight for people who are fostering, just for us to go along and talk to each other. Tomorrow there's the fostering committee. Wednesday is my night out with the girls, the childminders. On Thursday I've got friends coming round for dinner and on Friday there's a linen party. Saturday there's a benefit on. I also go to a gym twice a week. I'm going to be kept going all this week and I love that. When I don't have that, I get very down. That's why I feel I need a job which keeps me going. But I don't want to be a boss. I don't want to be in charge because I don't want to take decisions. I just want to be part of something, not the person who takes decisions.

It's a big responsibility having children. Their lives are in your hands. Now that they are older I'm looking forward to them taking responsibility for their own lives. I want to get a job which is more demanding and for the kids to live in their own homes and to visit. It's been a struggle but I don't regret anything. I don't want an awful lot out of life, just something to stimulate me, to keep me going, and perhaps one day to have a relationship.

A WOMAN'S RIGHT TO CHOOSE

BARBARA WALKER

'Any idiot can have babies'

My great-grandfather was a blacksmith's labourer and supported his wife and twelve children in a shared house in Hoxton, in London's East End. The Carmichael family downstairs also had twelve children. For my grandmother, escaping from the East End was a great dream and she admonished her only daughter with 'Any idiot can have babies, you get an education'. The war interrupted my mother's education and soon she was struggling with a sick husband, two young children and the poverty trap. In the pre-pill days, when I grew up, teenage sex was taboo and I was moulded in the work and education ethic so when I eventually did start work and became unintentionally pregnant, I had no qualms in choosing an abortion once I realised the father had bolted in horror.

I spent my 20s building a successful career and was a deputy head teacher within six years. I had experimented enough sexually to decide that relationships with women were more enjoyable than those with men and settled down with my first lesbian lover. Our relationship was to last for ten years. We enjoyed a fairly affluent lifestyle, travelled, became involved in the new wave lesbian politics and pretended not to be jealous when non-monogamy became the fashion. When we split up, we divided the household amicably and bought two flats next door to each other. Around that time other things were happening which led to further stress in my life: my father died and was buried while we were on holiday in Greece, I started a new job and my sister, already a single parent, had a severe post-natal depression after the birth of her second child. I stayed with her for a short while to help out with the housework and her 3-year-old son and the joy I experienced looking after the baby took me by surprise. Over the next month, as she found it impossible to cope, she asked if I would consider fostering my little niece, Jessie, and for the first time I imagined that life with a child would be exciting.

I realised that the demands of child-raising could now be met from my own resources and offered to bring Jessie up if negotiations with her father were fruitless and if my sister really wanted it. Painfully for us all, the baby died a few weeks later, but I shall always be grateful to her for bringing such a lot of good into my life. Although it wasn't too late to have my own child I realised that my emotional development had become stuck and I couldn't see the way forward, so I went to the Women's Therapy Centre. After a few courses there my confusion increased so I applied to the Tavistock Institute of Human Relations in the hope of being offered maybe one free session a week.

Instead, to my surprise, they diagnosed that I had a depressive illness and referred me to the Cassel Hospital, a psychotherapeutic community run without drugs on the NHS. Death and separation were only two of the issues I was to deal with and I arrived in a very crumpled state in my father's old car, with my niece's carrycot and clothes in the boot. I emerged a year later on a black and silver motorbike, full of energy for life. I was 35.

Bringing up a child was something I realised I would probably enjoy and do quite well. My former materialistic lifestyle seemed to be pointing to a dead end. I had sampled travel, sports, study, ambition at work, and sexual relationships. A future of doing more of the same felt vaguely undemanding. Ninety per cent of women have children and I believe the inherent drive to reproduce is a powerful one. As I could see my child-bearing years slipping away I became anxious that fate would deal a cruel blow and send me an early menopause. I was aware that a wrong decision now would mean years of regret later.

No return to the backstreets

Deciding how to become pregnant was the next step. The horror of the possibility of myself and the baby contracting AIDS immediately led me to rule out the option of a one-night stand. My hope was to give and care for life, not the opposite. Besides, I felt that women's rights to, for example, abortion had been won by bringing our needs out of the backstreets. Open and honest negotiation with a man therefore seemed the most positive way forward.

The first option I seriously, although only briefly, considered was to seek a long-term relationship with a suitable man. I didn't, however, want to confuse the search for a father for my child with the search for a live-in partner which in itself could be a lengthy process – and I didn't even know if I was still fertile. The second option, asking around gay and straight friends for a sperm-donor, proved fruitless. The third possibility was to use the anonymous donor network set up with a local anti-sexist men's group which believed in supporting a woman's right to choose how she becomes pregnant. A close friend in a long-term lesbian relationship had successfully used this network, although it had taken her two years to become pregnant, and she had spent many tense moments in traffic jams holding the precious donations close to her, warming the jar that contained them with a woolly sock. This arrangement of mutual anonymity was a direct result of judges ruling lesbians to be unfit mothers in custody cases in the seventies, as it seemed a sensible safeguard against possible unlooked for future interference by the donor.

I did, however, want to leave open the possibility of my child knowing her/his father, so, eventually, I settled for the fourth option of a known donor and placed two differently worded advertisements in *City Limits*. Within weeks I was gratefully sifting through thirty-eight replies. Discarding the offers from America and Scotland and the one about sexy suspenders, I worked my way through meetings with four unsuitable donors until I met John, a highly intelligent and sensitive man of my own age, who, as a market analyst, would appreciate the importance of delivery dates. We compared medical family histories and talked of possible ways of sharing the future. I had charted my mucus and temperature cycles and could, to my surprise and delight, pinpoint ovulation day with total accuracy.

The year I became pregnant there were 10,000 artificial insemination by donor births in the USA alone and I reasoned that, although my journey to pregnancy would appear out of the ordinary to some people, by the time my child grew up, the irrepressible tide of women's initiatives towards fulfilment would have widened the availability of choices around conception and motherhood still further.

Becoming a mother

One of my great heroines when I was deciding to have a baby was Dervla Murphy, who trekked 1,300 miles through the High Andes with her 9-year-old daughter and a donkey. Her achievements (or was it my image of her achievements?) kept me going for months.

Pregnancy was no problem physically until the tiredness set in near the end, when I pushed myself to keep working right up to the day Tom was born, so I could keep the maternity allowance to enjoy being at home with him afterwards. During the first months of pregnancy, I canoed down the River Wye, competed in the National Shearwater Sailing Races and backpacked alone around Mont Blanc (125 miles, 48,000 feet ascent and descent). On the negative side, however, was an unpleasant feeling of going in and out of an emotional hall of mirrors.

I shall always be grateful to my old school friend, Wendy, who offered to be my birth partner. We were an odd pair at the National Childbirth Trust class, especially when she had to join the men's group for some discussions. I think we may even have been mistakenly identified as a lesbian couple. My first lesbian lover, Teresa, agreed to be the other birth partner and when we eventually all ended up in the operating theatre for an epidural, episiotomy *and* emergency caesarian it was like a party. There was consultant Wendy Savage and her henchwoman duty doctor snipping and pulling at one end, and a woman anaesthetist and my two birth partners at the other, with a midwife and gay male nurse thrown in for good measure – and there was Tom held up in the lights for the first time. He was perfect. It was love at first sight.

Becoming a mother has meant experiencing a different area of the human struggle, so I have new concerns and different priorities. As a young childless teacher living and working in an area of urban decay, I was politically active around issues like violence to women, abortion, gay rights and equal opportunities. The shift in my personal world towards homebuilding, love for my own child and increased investment in the next generation finds me supporting organisations campaigning against homelessness, child abuse, international famine and disease and the destruction of the environment. Before, I would turn out at 5 am in the dark in thick snow to picket for the miners, whereas now I am not proud of the fact that I even neglected my own union membership this year and the support I do give to causes is mostly in sending cheques for small amounts from the comfort of my armchair.

Partly this change of concern is due to the emergence of new and urgent issues in the last few years. Wages for housework pales into insignificance when faced with pictures of twenty million people short of food in the Horn of Africa. Partly the change illustrates for me how clearly politics is linked to organising around self-interest and neatly debunks any sanctimonious occupation of moral high ground by activists. Partly getting to any meeting is so difficult now, having to take into consideration my tiredness, finding a babysitter, and whether Tom should be left. It is frustrating to be thought of as a complacent oldster by young, childless teachers leading the kind of life that I used to lead.

As a single woman, the wars of the 1980s left me fairly uninvolved but, as the mother of a male child in the context of the Gulf War, I was deeply horrified by the anguish of mothers and their children in Iraq and Kuwait and appalled at the suffering that families endure when adult men go to war. Yet I can now envisage supporting physical violence in defence of what is so precious to me, and a further paradox is that I would not want *my* son to go to war.

One unexpected positive result of motherhood, with all its contradictions, is that I do feel generally more rooted in that I can now relate to a larger number of women and men who also carry the burden of child-rearing responsibilities. From those early days when I was fêted with gifts and congratulations in the maternity ward, I realised that I was entering into a new relationship with the community. As I was waved down the hospital steps surrounded by friends and whisked away in a high status car to a champagne homecoming, I remember thinking that this is what it must be like to get married.

From being a single, childless lesbian in a position systematically marginalised by society, it seemed that I was suddenly being received everywhere by warm smiling faces. As a sportswoman or motorcyclist, a lesbian, teacher or single woman, I can remember receiving verbal abuse, ridicule, criticism and discouragement from all sorts of hecklers and members of the general public. Now I am a mother such harassers have gone strangely quiet. Instead, a supermarket trip with Tom as a small baby became a jolly social outing as complete strangers lined the aisles to talk to me, eager to share and relive memories of their own early motherhood. Older women told me what I shouldn't be letting my child touch on the shelves, and offered various other forms of advice. All this was a surprise and reminded me in part of the time I went in fancy dress as a clown to the children's Christmas dinner at the school where I was teaching. To be greeted with universal affection is very uplifting but of course is only a change in outward appearance. I was now enjoying the sanctified image of mother and child, totally safe and totally under control.

In the countryside of East London

Tom is 4 now and I am 44. We live together with an ageing and much loved samoyed dog, Jezzie, in our own small terraced house on the edge of Walthamstow Marshes by the River Lea in East London. This unploughed wild marshland is a ninety-acre site of special scientific interest and teems with wildlife, so we can watch the foxes run along the railway line at the bottom of our garden at night, watch for the return of the cuckoo, swifts and frog spawn in spring, search for adders, tongue fern among the sedges and fill our lungs with breathable air in the evening while watching bats and flights of geese return from feeding on the Thames mudflats. I am very pleased that I have been able to make a secure home for us here and that there will be plenty of educational, cultural and sporting opportunities around as Tom grows up.

The cost of this security is having to live more of a mono-cultural life based around working longer hours than I would prefer. Fortunately I enjoy my work as a specialist music teacher in schools five miles away and it has been easy to shape my working week around Tom's changing needs. For the first six months I was at home with him just working on Saturday mornings and when the maternity benefit and the £1,000 'Baby Fund' that I had saved dried up, I found a babyminder so that I could do two days work a week. Overhead costs on our tiny flat were low and I was lucky to have a low interest, fixed-rate mortgage, a good network of friends, offers to babysit and time to enjoy being together. I even enjoyed rehearsing and performing at local community events with a women's steel band which was personally very satisfying, especially when Tom was there too, bobbing about on my back in the baby carrier.

Although in selling my flat at the end of the house price

boom in 1988 I released another £1,000, the increase in bills at the new house, inflation and the £200 per month baby-minding fees, soon meant that my working week had to extend into the evenings and weekends with private teaching. For the next two years during termtime I was often numb with exhaustion and became more isolated as the work timetable cut through the usual hours when people get together.

I bought equipment second-hand, ate a lot of cheese sandwiches, and gratefully received large sacks of toddler clothes from friends. During the holidays it was a relief to grow back together again. We visited friends and I could spend some time just enjoying being with Tom and watching all those precious toddler activities like putting pebbles in puddles.

Holidays didn't equal relaxation, however, as I always used part of them to tackle as many exterior and interior house and car repairs as I could, as it is much cheaper to do them myself, so I often found that I was returning to work having had little respite.

Now Tom has started in the nursery at the school where I teach, I can see a lot more physical and economic freedom in the coming year and I plan to reduce my workload and overdraft accordingly, so life should become less stressed for both of us. Tom learns fast, is confident, helpful, considerate, intelligent and well liked and I am confident too that I am a good provider and a 'good enough' mother.

Stereotypes

The circle of people I come into contact with are usually encouraging and complimentary and, of course, some are single parents themselves or were brought up by single parents. It wasn't until recently when I started to focus on the broader public response to single parents that I realised there were so many hostile criticisms being made of us. My first observation about this response must be that any generalisations about single parents are difficult to make because we are present in so many conditions of society and for some it is just a transitory lifestyle. We have also arrived at the position from many different directions. If there are negative images in people's minds in general, they probably stem partly from the fact that almost half of single parent families live on the poverty line compared with six per cent of married couples with children. If asked about what it means to be a single parent, a superficial response might mention wailing children, exhausted young women and piles of dirty washing. This, of course, is a good description of most of my married friends trying to bring up their children, pay the mortgage and work outside the home.

It is not only poverty in itself, however, that some people seem to object to but the two-fold social 'crime' of being a drain on the national economy and of being unhealthily dependent on handouts by accepting social security payments. I have found this a fairly complex area to unravel. Very few people make these criticisms directly to me and a comment like, 'Did you know my father thinks single parents are the cause of all the problems in society?' casually made on a Sunday afternoon walk, leaves me boxing with shadows. Was this just scapegoating or does this father fear his own dependency feelings? Is it the fast pace of post-industrial change that makes him feel he is losing control and leaves him wanting to revert to the security of past conditions and does he feel rejected by images of women looking to the state for baseline security and avoiding more male-centred lives? He may well feel his past struggles and achievements for his own family are devalued by other people 'getting it easier' and I suspect that his work and social life will have bypassed any real contact with either single parents or people who struggle with downward spirals of poverty. With 164,000 decrees absolute given in the UK in 1989, and given that two thirds of divorced husbands subsequently lose all contact with their children, it seems to me that anyone who censures the single parent who *does* fulfil a commitment to the children must be either thoughtless, perverse or a bigotted misogynist.

Although the broad front of criticism against single parents does not sway my personal beliefs or decision-making directly, there are ways in which my life is affected. Critics use their political vote to put in power a party which does not advance my lifestyle in its philosophy or policies. For example, the political right does not want to promote single parenthood or working mothers and will pay for and report on research which 'proves' that children who have been cared for by babyminders will find making sustained relationships in adult life impossible. It has brought in new anti-gay legislation, and newspapers aligned to the right sell copies by headlining stories of women loving each other. It discusses issues like surrogacy in terms of 'prostitution of fertility' rather than delighting in the joy children can bring to those who long for them. It has brought in legislation resulting in a situation where single women are now afraid that the new regulations applied to infertility clinics will make it difficult for them to gain access to artificial insemination by donor. The alarm of a Scottish baroness in the House of Lords that an anonymous donor creeping into a family pedigree would give rise to a fake clan chief epitomises for me the establishment's concern about property and inheritance in the context of the traditional family.

All this means that when I meet someone for the first time I can never be sure whether their initial friendly response will evaporate or, worse still, turn to disgust when they discover that I am a lesbian single parent and that Tom was conceived as a result of advertising for a sperm donor in *City Limits*. I begrudge the energy it has taken from my life to work against this flow and feel frustrated that I can do so little at the moment to fight for what I believe in. Prejudice is integral to an unjust and unequal society and I feel angry that the refusal to share wealth has played its part in a steady increase in crimes of hate in the home and on the street. Last winter, when Tom and I came face to face with an old woman – a heap of filthy skin and bones – lying on the hard pavement in a snow storm outside London's multi-million-pound Broad Street development, I felt deeply ashamed of the society in which I live and didn't know what to say to my bewildered little boy.

When politicians and others talk of single parents as young unmarried mothers scrounging on the state they are proliferating stereotypes. Such distortions seem to be used most when there is a lack of any real knowledge about a social group and some are so persistent that proliferators must have an interest in maintaining them. I have been confused by such distortions in searching over the years for my real self and have half believed in some of them, despite daily seeing the evidence disproving them, under my nose.

Some of the hardest stereotypes to supplant are those I was indoctrinated with as a child and they are associated with taboo, prejudice and a closed mind, so I am mindful about this as Tom grows.

Communities?

In trying to break the moulds in my own mind, I have also had to throw out a lot of ideas which were built around fantasies of group identity which had seemed at the time to offer a welcome security. For example, the way I thought about the lesbian community after the first national lesbian conference in 1976 was confused because it didn't look the way I hoped it would. Many women were shouting and few listening. In the hurry to change people's minds, the truth was foreshortened and yet the lesbian cause demanded loyalty which I was happy to give. I would say now that loyalty is hard to maintain without reciprocal support. When a lesbian at a party recently called Tom a mutant, behind my back of course, and my part in the lesbian baby boom is seen by some writers in the gay press as taking care and support away from lesbians, my 'female energy being sucked into caretaking more boys', I still feel I don't fit in with this ideal community

I have partly invented, and partly been fed in stereotypical form, by the need to appear unified in order to campaign successfully.

These days the people Tom and I spend time with and enjoy being with are those whose diverse lifestyles and interests are yet compatible enough to make worthwhile the effort to arrange to meet. Whether we are Black, bisexual, single, or part of a couple, doesn't seem to matter as much as whether we would enjoy some company at the swimming-pool or park, or, after a busy week, catching up with each other's news over a cup of tea or gin and tonic. More objectively, our friends are usually liberal-minded, value education and struggle to make ends meet, although most are employed.

One outing in particular stands out from last year as illustrating our positive experiences of companionship. Four of us, single mothers, had travelled down from London to Horstead Keynes in Sussex with our five children, for a bluebell picnic and ride on the preserved steam railway. As we relaxed after sharing each other's food and the children played happily in the nearby stream, I watched an unpleasant scene developing in a Mini in the car park where driver dad was haranging map-reading mum and both ended up shouting at their two children in the back seat. This brought back so many memories of claustrophobic nuclear family rows for me that, in contrast, the space and light between the members of our party positively seemed to glow. *We* could all drive and map read at the same time. Living alone with our children, the adults in our party had sought out each other's company freely and the day's activities unfolded with common consent and respect. The number of social interactions possible with nine people made for an interesting day and a group can probably cope better with any individual mood swings. It wasn't until a long while after that I realised what a wide variety of experiences we and our children had brought with us that day – gay and straight, divorced and unmarried, different ethnic and social backgrounds – and our children are growing up boys and girls in a society radically different from the one experienced by each of their parents. As a group we certainly don't live in each other's pockets, but we generally get together to enjoy the year's cycle of holidays and celebrations.

As for my family, my mother has been a steady support to Tom and he loves her dearly. My father died fifteen years ago and my mother's second husband was a very loving grandfather generously sharing his passion for steam trains and model making for a short while before he too died when Tom was 3.

Relationships within my original family were never easy and my mother and I had practically severed ours before Tom was born. My mother's feeling about the birth was one of being excluded and mine was that it was too stressful to involve her. Since then we have gradually constructed a stable truce based on a shared love for Tom. We visit for short periods and Tom loves staying with her for an occasional weekend in Norfolk. She enjoys watching him grow. We also enjoy visits with my elderly aunt and her daughter's family in London. That is our total family involvement, which is very different from the tribe of grandparents, great aunts and uncles and cousins and their children who used to come and go during my early years.

During the early meetings with Tom's father, John, we discussed possibilities for a creatively shared future. These evaporated when he disappeared the day after Tom was born. Since then he has resurfaced and disappeared three times in four years and has proved to have a more immature personality than I originally allowed for. For my part, I was naïve to allow myself to fantasise on the basis of early conversations and the external trappings of education, accent, high IQ, briefcase and high-powered job. Under all that he was just another man looking for a mother/wife for himself and not any of the adult experiences of fatherhood. Some of my friends who are involved in stressful conflicts with the fathers of their children envy the idea of such an absence. It wasn't what I had hoped or planned for, but I can adapt to reality once the facts become clear and I hope Tom will have that ability too.

After years of trying to re-establish contact I did eventually arrange a meeting in Devon for the three of us. I did this partly because of all the published work which points to the importance of children finding and experiencing their roots and partly to find out the reality of John's situation.

It is obviously important to remain aware and open to the question of roots and identity. Too much anxiety on my part could create a self-fulfilling problem, just as too little concern could be a pitfall. I am very aware of the current philosophy in this culture to 'sell' the father's essential goodness to the child so that it becomes incorporated in a positive self-image. Books and experts can be very wrong but a few weeks before the meeting Tom made a passing remark as the clouds were gathering and darkening one night when we were walking the dog. He referred to a dark monster in the park being his daddy.

Since the meeting with John a few things have been clearer. The first surprising result was that I felt a new freedom to take the credit for successfully bringing up Tom alone. John's life seems less 'together' than mine at the moment and he has begun therapy, looking at abuse in his own childhood. Far from sitting on a fortune while we have been struggling, he has managed on a student grant and then a salary half that of mine. I am sure we haven't seen the last of him and would welcome further contact. Although I now don't feel the perplexed sadness, the bitter disappointment or the anger I felt when he first disappeared, I still get emotionally involved when discussing the performance of fathers in general in society. The second result of the meeting is that the dark monster has never been seen again. We did see a little dog one afternoon, however, in the middle of a big field, which was 'A daddy all on its ownly'.

With few relatives on one side and almost none on the other, fortunately we are free to choose friends who are very important to us, and, to a lesser extent, neighbours who are a friendly and positive part of our lives.

Learning by experience

It took me many years to realise that lesbians are everywhere and can be titled or tattoed, soldiers, midwives, criminals or doctors. On the whole I have stopped assuming from people's outward appearances either what their contribution to society is likely to be or how at ease they feel about their identity. It is these last two factors which I believe to be the key issues governing Tom's future happiness. I enjoy encouraging and providing opportunities for his emotional, physical, spiritual and intellectual growth as best I can. He goes to dance class, swims regularly with friends, enjoys gymnastics and cycling and we always spend several weeks each year at our old caravan on the sand dunes in a remote part of the Norfolk coast, communing with nature and friends who come to visit with their tents. We enjoy sledging, flying kites, gardening and blackberrying as the seasons come and go and, of course, he attends an excellent school. I tell him often how proud I am of him, how happy he makes me and how I will always love him.

Despite all I can do, it is inevitable that one day he will meet up with some of society's censorious attitudes to homosexuality. Our local council decided last year to encourage gay men and lesbians to come forward as possible foster parents but met with minority vociferous opposition. One Tory Councillor declared, 'I am not prepared to deliver the children of this borough into the hands of filthy perverts.' I hope that Tom will not be hurt or divided by such attitudes. So far, the issue of having a lesbian mum is a latent one as I have not had a lover since I was pregnant so neither he nor I have had to deal with my adult sexuality in its new context. He stays regularly with his beloved 'Auntie Treesie' and her lover, Barbara, and it is part of his natural world that they sometimes sleep together, not an 'unnatural passion' at all.

Most people living worthwhile, fulfilled lives are happy to

get on with them and for others to do the same, but I am very familiar with situations at school where the seeds of conflict are continuously sown by a few children who feel bad about themselves and want to project their negative feelings on to other children. Fortunately the school that Tom attends and where I teach, has up-to-date policies and confronts issues like bullying, racism and dealing with conflict, so that these things do not get in the way of learning as much as they might. Moreover, although there are of course occasional problems which disturb the calm, there are enough supportive, kind children, who are often very considerate to each other, to make it a very pleasant place to be.

Hopes

There were times soon after Tom was born when I would really have liked to share my joy at every little thing he did with someone equally indulgent, but being a single parent also means having the luxury of the complete freedom to explore being the kind of mother I want to be.

My two greatest hopes are for Tom's happiness and that we will stay the best of friends for many years to come. I hope he will have a personality with a secure core, with less guilt, and therefore less resentment, and more happiness in his growing years than I had; less forbidden enquiry, less isolation and less fear of expressing his feelings.

A young male psychiatrist once told me that a child needs two parents. He seemed to have an irrationally fixed idea about the quantity rather than the quality of parenting. If I believed that the traditional family of mum, dad and 1.8 children was the only guaranteed recipe for success, then I would have to admit that I had been selfish in deciding to have a child on my own. But this so obviously is not the truth that there is no case to answer. Who are the people who call single women who choose to parent selfish? Certainly none of my friends, colleagues or acquaintances, all of whom say admiringly that they don't think they could take on the hard work involved. It was partly because I felt that my life had become too self-centred that I could wholeheartedly throw myself into motherhood. Having found myself, explored myself and enjoyed myself when I was younger, I could put self aside and enjoy providing for someone else's dependency.

Many philosophies accept that it is a human condition to avoid pain and choose pleasure. If being selfish is choosing what will give us most pleasure, then most humans are selfish and I am no more or less selfish than any other mother whose child gives her great pleasure. I believe emotional bonding between mother and child is above words like selfish and that every woman has a right to reproduce if she can and chooses to. I hope that women will increasingly be able to exercise the kind of choices which I have made.